Designing Writing Assignments

Designing Writing Assignments

Traci Gardner
National Council of Teachers of English

National Council of Teachers of English
1111 W. Kenyon Road, Urbana, Illinois 61801-1096

Student handouts throughout this book appear in, or were adapted from, lesson plans on the ReadWriteThink website (http://www.readwritethink.org) and are used by permission. Part of Verizon's Thinkfinity, ReadWriteThink is a nonprofit website maintained by the National Council of Teachers of English and the International Reading Association, with support from the Verizon Foundation. The site publishes free lesson plans, interactive student materials, Web resources, and standards for classroom teachers of reading and the English language arts.

Staff Editor: Becky Standard

Interior Design: Doug Burnett

Cover Design: Frank P. Cucciarre, Blink Concept & Design, Inc.

Cover Photos: ©2008 Jupiterimages Corporation

NCTE Stock Number: 10850

Library of Congress Cataloging-in-Publication Data

Gardner, Traci.
    Designing writing assignments/Traci Gardner.
        p. cm.
    Includes bibliographical references.
        ISBN 978-0-8141-1085-0 (pbk.)
    1. English language—Composition and exercises—Study and teaching—United States. 2. English language—Rhetoric—Study and teaching—United States. I. National Council of Teachers of English. II. Title.
PE1405.U6G37 2008
808'.042071—dc22

2007047467

For my father and mother

Charles and Patti Gardner

Contents

Acknowledgments

Thank you to my wonderful colleagues here at NCTE for tolerating all those days when I was hiding in my cubicle, banging away furiously at the keyboard. Kurt Austin, Bonny Graham, Cari Rich, Margaret Chambers, and Zarina Hock read many drafts and kindly shepherded me through the writing and publication process. Sharon Roth, Lisa Fink, and Scott Filkins carved out time in our busy ReadWriteThink schedule to allow me to pursue my dream of writing a book.

Thank you to Hugh Burns, Wayne Butler, Fred Kemp, Nancy Peterson, John Slatin, and Paul Taylor, my colleagues and friends from the Daedalus Group, for originally supporting the Lists of Ten when I proposed them, and especially to Daedalus friends Locke Carter and Becky Rickly, for believing in me even when I don't believe in myself.

Thank you to my colleagues on the TechRhet, WPA-L, and EngTeach-Talk discussion lists for embracing the Lists of Ten over the many years that I have published them.

Thank you to Will Banks, Samantha Blackmon, Eric Crump, Michael Day, Jim Kalmbach, and John Paul Walter, for encouraging me before I even figured out what I was writing and for continuing to be cheerleaders through the entire process.

Thank you to Cynthia Y. Selfe, Richard Selfe, and Cheryl Ball, for giving me the time, space, and support to write during CIWIC all those summers. You provided me with the most wonderful, supportive environment and always told me I could do it.

Finally, love and thank you to my family—Patti, Charles, Holli, Kerri, Noel, Kelli, Eryk, Randy, and Hunter.

Introduction

As writing teachers, we rely on writing assignments. Paper, pens and pencils, computers, highlighters, dictionaries, and a thesaurus—all are resources we'd ask students to use as they compose a text. But before any of that, there's a writing assignment. Even if we tell students to write about anything they want, we have still given them an assignment. Writing assignments are, in many ways, the structure that holds a writing class together.

Because these assignments have such a significant role, designing them is one of our most important jobs. So much depends upon the writing assignments that we ask students to complete: they can set the tone for a course, address multiple goals in the classroom, and influence students' engagement. And yet, most of us have at one time or another presented students with an assignment designed at the last minute, moments before class starts. I know I have—and I know it can be hard not to do so occasionally because of all the demands we face in (and out of) the classroom. Designing writing assignments is just one of the many tasks that we must complete as we teach, and of those tasks, designing writing assignments is one of the more complicated jobs that we face.

Writing teachers face challenges similar to those that students face when composing a writing assignment. We have to identify audience, purpose, and voice. We have to decide on the best structure and format. We have to determine the time frame and point out the resources that will help students complete the assignment. Clearly, composing writing assignments is no simple charge. Edward M. White explains this challenge: "The construction of appropriate writing assignments is one of the hardest jobs for the teacher . . . and is exacerbated by the dearth of supportive material available. Every teacher should keep in mind that designing assignments is a particularly demanding form of *writing*, calling for the teacher to use the entire writing process, most particularly revision with an eye to the audience. Careful consideration of the needs of the audience for the assignment and class discussion of the assignment, over the entire period when students are working on it, will help the teacher find out where the students are having problems; reflection about these problems will often lead to a revised assignment for future classes" (8). The important concept here is that when teachers design writing assignments, they are engaging in a "form of writing." Perhaps this fact is obvious, and yet ineffective writing assignments probably result more from insufficient attention to the rhetorical demands of this composing process than from anything else.

As we begin our design task, we may first think of the many questions that each assignment requires us to answer:

- What is the task?
- When is it due?
- How long should it be?
- Does it need to result in a typed and double-spaced document?
- Does it need a cover page?
- Is research necessary? If so, how much?
- Where can writers find help?
- Is a multimodal text acceptable?
- What needs to be turned in? Is a rough draft required?
- How will the resulting text(s) be graded?

Since the answers to these questions can be different for every class, if not for every student, the assignments we create need to include as many options for fulfilling the requirements as possible.

Even if we answer all these questions, however, we still have a great deal of work to do to create a strong writing assignment, because designing one is much more complex than just answering a list of questions. We must balance pedagogical and curricular goals with the needs of multiple learners with multiple abilities, all within the context of the resources available in our classrooms. Adding to this complexity are local, state, and federal standards, mandated assessment and testing programs, and the realities of our workloads.

These complicated intersections result in a demanding rhetorical situation that can place the needs of individual learners at odds with the more generic goals of the curriculum. How can we encourage student autonomy and still address all the demands placed on our classes and students? If we provide students with a range of options, how can we support all learners and ensure that mandated goals are met? This book explores the answers to these questions and provides examples —as well as a "Lesson Plan" icon in the margin when there are related lesson plans on the ReadWriteThink website (http://www.readwritethink.org)—that demonstrate how teachers can meet such challenges in the writing classroom.

1 The Essentials of an Effective Writing Assignment

I know that good writing assignments result in good writing. I've seen the ways that writers—me, my colleagues, my classmates, the students whom I've taught—write stronger, more sophisticated papers when they are asked to respond to well-developed writing assignments.

When I first started teaching business writing, for instance, I tried the very basic assignments included in many of the texts I had reviewed. These assignments were often totally bare-bones: "Write a fund-raising letter" or "Write a bad-news memo." Totally bare-bones—and totally ineffective. Neither of these prompts gives students the support and information they need to successfully complete the writing task. Such assignments are not limited to the business writing classroom of course. In a language arts or composition classroom, they take the form of prompts such as "Write a persuasive essay" or "Write an analysis of the novel." When I presented students with such stripped-down assignments, they typically wrote extremely general responses with unclear purposes and audiences. Compare these generic prompts with the following assignment:

> There has been a problem in Montgomery County Schools with discipline and violence. On the basis of the positive examples that they have seen at other Virginia schools, Families for Safe Schools, a local community group, is calling for the school board to adopt a school uniform policy in order to cut down on these problems. What is your position on this issue? Write a letter to the editor of a local newspaper or the school newspaper, stating your position on this issue and supporting it with convincing reasons. Turn in two copies of your letter and an envelope addressed to the newspaper (I'll provide the stamp). I'll grade one copy and send the other copy off to the newspaper.

When I used this assignment—one that offers considerable support and detail—students responded with stronger writing. I quickly learned that the more detail and attention I put into the writing assignments, the better students' writing was.

It's not that I was just lucky. Research tells us that student success in the writing classroom is directly related to the support and direction provided in the assignments. Barbara A. Storms, Anastasia Riazantseva, and Claudia Gentile analyzed the writing that students completed for the 1998 National Assessment for Educational Progress (NAEP) Special Study on Classroom Writing for a 2000 NAEP/ETS report. This examination, as reported in *California English,* began with the following observation: "The students had obviously spent class periods working on the assignment. The topics were very similar, yet the results very different. In both classes, students had written drafts, talked with other students and/or the teacher about their writing, then rewritten their pieces to a 'final' product. Yet one set of papers was lively and well written; the kind of papers where readers wondered what would come next and were disappointed when the last paper in the set had been read. The other class's papers were predictable, each one sounding similar to the next. What made the written products differ so greatly?" (26).

The critical difference was the writing assignments. Storms, Riazantseva, and Gentile found that writing assignments that offered students the chance to engage with the available information on a topic and then make their own analyses, reflections, observations, or syntheses resulted in stronger writing. In addition to the importance of the content of the assignment, they found that "stronger pieces resulted when writing was a genuine act of communication" (26). As they close their discussion of the study, the researchers state that "qualities of writing assignments strongly influenced the writing outcomes" (27).

A 2001 NAEP/National Writing Project study drew similar conclusions about the relationship between writing assignments and the success of student writers. The study looked at writing assignments and the related writing that students composed, as well as at interview transcripts of both students and teachers reflecting on the assignments. A second, related study analyzed the writing assignments that led to the strongest student writing. The study found that the most effective writing assignments paid attention to these essential characteristics:

- The *content and scope* asked students to focus on critical thinking, rather than reiteration, by interacting with a text.
- The *organization and development* provided scaffolding that supported students' writing process.

- The *audience* for the assignment focused on *communication* with an authentic group of readers regarding a topic on which the writer was an expert.

- A range of *choices* for students' focus was balanced with support and direction so that students could *engage* in the process as equal partners, rather than be directed to complete teacher-driven tasks. (Peterson)

The report stresses that "these characteristics of strong assignments can not [*sic*] be seen in isolation; they are interconnected." In other words, an effective writing assignment must include all of these components in an integrated and relevant way.

For students to succeed, research and, often, our own experience tell us that the writing assignments we create must fulfill all these requirements. The essential elements of an effective writing assignment may seem quite obvious. Students should be asked to engage in higher-level writing that focuses on interpretation, analysis, and synthesis. They should be given support that encourages a multidraft composing process. Students should be experts on the topics that they write about, and they should be asked to engage with a group of real, known readers. Students should be able to choose from several options for each project.

Even students tell us that they need writing tasks that fit these criteria. The problem is that often we don't hear them. Look at the typical resources on designing writing assignments that are widely available online and in various articles and books. Without too much searching, you'll find assertions such as this one, from Northern Illinois University's Writing Across the Curriculum program: "Students often complain that they don't know what the teacher wants. Even though we may be quite explicit in describing the writing assignment, students will tend to forget details unless the assignment is in print." The solution, according to this site, is to provide students with an assignment sheet that explains such details as the kind of writing required, its scope and length, the formatting requirements, and the due dates. Even when we provide these details, however, "students may still claim that they don't know what the teacher wants"; this resource suggests that teachers provide additional support materials to help avoid students' complaints.

Students do complain—I've certainly heard my share of student dissatisfaction. It's not surprising that teachers get frustrated when we're asked to explain an activity for the umpteenth time. Comments like these from Northern Illinois University's website feel natural, perhaps even justified. Yet, the language also reveals what can go wrong when we present assignments to students.

The language introducing these tips and heuristics blames the students—rhetorically, the readers of these assignments—for problems in the composition classroom: Students complain. Students forget. Students *claim* they don't know what we want. This kind of language places students very obviously at fault. Teachers, it seems, or the writing assignments themselves, are blameless.

Yet in these same classrooms, we urge students to analyze their audience and provide enough details for their readers to understand the messages in their texts. We urge them to accept that readers cannot guess what an author means, so writers must work diligently to communicate clearly. Our own knowledge of the composition process, in other words, should lead us to fit our writing assignments to the specific group of readers in the classroom—to fit the message to the audience's needs.

The research by Storms, Riazantseva, and Gentile as well as the findings of the 2001 NAEP/National Writing Project study indicate that writing assignments need to contain adequate detail for students to understand and accomplish the writing task. We need to match the writing assignments we give students with their needs as developing writers. Unfortunately, there is frequently a wide gap in meaning between what students read into a writing assignment and what the teacher means and wants.

Members of the University of Hawaii Mānoa Writing Program interviewed over 200 students in writing intensive courses over a two-year period for its *Writing Matters #1* newsletter. These interviews revealed the gaps between students' and teachers' visions of writing tasks. As an example, one teacher in the program expressed this expectation:

> For the short paper on a video, I wanted students to make connections among the archeologist's questions, the methods used to get answers, and principles from their reading.

Compare that expectation with what a student who was interviewed understood:

> This assignment was like writing a high-school movie review. I wanted to give my own personal understanding about the video, so I was going to write a narrative.

On the basis of such examples, the researchers found that students typically "translate an instructor's goals into processes they think they can handle." Here, the student focuses on "personal understanding" and narrative writing, rather than on the more sophisticated analysis and synthesis that the instructor expected. Additionally, the researchers determined that students frequently rely on techniques and strategies used in earlier assignments (in this case a high-school movie review) "rather than risk something new."

The Mānoa Writing Program interviews reveal three different versions of the assignment in play. In *Teaching Literature as Reflective Practice*, Kathleen Blake Yancey explains that there are three curricula in the classroom: the lived curriculum, the delivered curriculum, and the experienced curriculum (16–17). The relationships among these three curricula can inform our understanding of how writing assignments affect students' success as writers. The lived curriculum, "the curriculum that students bring in the door with them" (16), is clear in this student's reference to "a high-school movie review." That prior knowledge affected the way that this student approached the writing assignment. The delivered curriculum, "the one [teachers] design" (17), is evident in the assignment that the teacher presented to the class—the directive to write a short analytical video review that connected to class readings. The experienced curriculum, "the curriculum that *students construct* in the context of both the lived curriculum they bring with them and the delivered curriculum [teachers] seek to share" (58), is something of a mash-up of the prior knowledge and experiences from the lived curriculum, artifacts from the delivered curriculum, and the interpretations students make as they work in a course. The student interview shows the experienced curriculum, which is based on an interpretation of the delivered assignment and prior experience with movie reviews: "I wanted to give my own personal understanding about the video, so I was going to write a narrative." In the places where these three curricula overlap, student learning can occur, and students are more likely to meet teachers' expectations for a course. Where there are gaps between students' interpretations and the delivered assignment, however, the result can be unsatisfactory student writing.

Our understanding of reading and cognitive processes can explain why the delivered curriculum and the experienced curriculum can be so different. Reading is always a process of interpreting a text. Based on their prior knowledge and experience, readers cast the ideas in a text to match their own understanding of its concepts. In their explanation of how students read, David Bartholomae and Anthony Petrosky explain: "The question is not, then, whether some students' readings miss the mark. All readings are misses. The key question, as [Jonathan] Culler says, is 'whose misses matter,' and these decisions depend upon a 'host of complex and contingent factors,' factors that help 'one to question the institutional forces and practices that institute the normal by marking or excluding the deviant'" (6). Because all readers come to a text with different experiences and prior knowledge, all readings are different— and none is absolutely identical to the writer's original intentions. Knowing that there is always a difference between readers and writers, Bartholomae and Petrosky urge teachers to consider how power and authority influence these divergent understandings. Some readings are close enough to the author's intention, while others wander far from the original purpose. In the case of the latter, the question becomes not whether the reader understands but whether the reader understands adequately enough for the text to achieve its purpose.

In the classroom, differences between the delivered curriculum and the experienced one stem from students' construction, or reading, of the classroom in general and of the writing assignment in particular. Every writing assignment is a multifaceted text composed of specific artifacts (such as handouts and peer review guidelines), peer and teacher feedback on current and previous writing, social interaction in and out of class, and students' personal experiences. In her 1990 case study of thirteen students, Jennie Nelson concludes that students' readings of a text directly affect their performance: "It seems important for teachers to know that students actively interpret the assignments they receive, and that students often rely on implicit cues to determine what counts in completing tasks. These case studies suggest that students' task interpretations are based, at least in part, on situational factors over which the teacher has some control—namely, the criteria used to evaluate products, the quality and frequency of feedback, and the nature of the instructions and other explicit support students receive for completing assignments" (391). Simple delivery of assignment artifacts is not enough. To design successful writing assignments, teachers must attend to the situational factors Nelson identifies in ways that build overlap between the experienced curriculum and the delivered curriculum. In other words, they must expand the writing assignment in ways that help students construct a reading that matches the goals for the activity. In doing so, they widen the overlap between the delivered curriculum and the experienced one.

Consider the gaps that can occur because of the language used in writing assignments. Assignment prompts typically engage in the language of academic discourse and ask student writers not only to complete a writing task but also to complete a task that is explained in language that may not be familiar to them and may recall various previous writing experiences. Jim Burke describes the predicament students can face:

> Academic words like "compare" and "evaluate," "argument" and "claim," come with their own academic connotations; they are concepts, habits of mind, ways of thinking that are not intuitive. Indeed, many terms, such as "argument," come with their own conventions. Thus to ask students to "write a short essay in which you make a claim about the author's purpose" is to introduce several concepts students must learn to "unpack" if they are to write what the assignment demands.
>
>   These words are consequential: if students do not understand them, they will not achieve success on class assignments, tests, or state exams. (37, 39)

Even when an assignment calls for the higher-level critical thinking that studies have identified as crucial to improved student writing, students may not read the writing task in ways that actually lead to the expected critical thinking. We must, as Burke explains, "unpack" the meanings and construct a shared reading of the activity.

When teachers and students explore their readings of writing tasks openly and actively, the experienced curriculum that students construct is more likely to result in strong writing. On the basis of a deeper reading of four case studies from her original research, Jennie Nelson, in "Reading Classrooms as Text: Exploring Student Writers' Interpretive Practices," identifies the value of paying attention to students' readings of the curriculum: "This finding underscores the value of exploring students' interpretive practices, of understanding how the set of assumptions about school writing that students invoke each time they undertake a writing assignment complicates our best efforts and most innovative assignments. It also underscores the importance of finding ways to make students' interpretive practices a part of the classroom discussion about writing assignments" (427). Thought of in light of this research, a writing assignment is far more than a handout listing a prompt and various deadlines. The text of a writing assignment must also involve what Kathleen Blake Yancey describes as "inviting [the] experienced curriculum into the course, making it visible and thus accessible and indeed legitimate" (*Teaching* 17). The delivered curriculum must provide pathways that connect prior experiences (the lived curriculum) and students' interpretations (the experienced curriculum) directly with the teacher's expectations. When these three curricula overlap in our construction of writing assignments, we are better able to support student writers by scaffolding their comprehension of the task.

The success of a writing assignment hinges on our definition of one. The term *writing assignment* must be synonymous with a full process that includes creating explanatory materials, defining a task that touches on the four key areas outlined in the NWP/NAEP study, explaining and exploring the expectations for the activity, and pointing out available support. By paying attention to the entire process, we can ensure that the assignments we devise or choose for students contribute to their success as writers.

2 Putting Beliefs into Practice

We know the basic characteristics of an effective writing assignment, but where do we begin the process of composing such assignments? Before we address any concerns we may have about logistics, form, style, or content, we need to begin with our pedagogical understanding of writers and how they write. We have to be aware of our beliefs as teachers of writing.

In November 2004, the Writing Study Group of the NCTE Executive Committee published the "NCTE Beliefs about the Teaching of Writing" (see the Appendix). This NCTE guideline outlines eleven beliefs about the way people develop writing abilities:

1. Everyone has the capacity to write, writing can be taught, and teachers can help students become better writers.

2. People learn to write by writing.

3. Writing is a process.

4. Writing is a tool for thinking.

5. Writing grows out of many different purposes.

6. Conventions of finished and edited texts are important to readers and therefore to writers.

7. Writing and reading are related.

8. Writing has a complex relationship to talk.

9. Literate practices are embedded in complicated social relationships.

10. Composing occurs in different modalities and technologies.

11. Assessment of writing involves complex, informed, human judgment.

By applying these principles to what we know about effective writing assignments, we can ensure that our writing assignments provide the resources students need to become better writers.

Each of the following points in the "NCTE Beliefs" contributes to a more complete understanding of the characteristics of effective writing assignments. If we take them one at a time, we can explore exactly how these beliefs influence each assignment we design.

1. Everyone has the capacity to write, writing can be taught, and teachers can help students become better writers.

Perhaps this belief seems obvious. I know I believe that writing can be taught—I am a writing teacher after all. I've taught writing for over twenty years, and I've seen student writers improve and learn new strategies and skills. If we are to teach writing, we need to believe that writing can be taught. The challenge for us as we design writing assignments is to find the most effective way to accomplish that goal. It's not just a matter of believing that "teachers can help students become better writers." We have to recognize *how* teachers help student writers improve and learn, and we then have to use that knowledge to shape the tasks and support systems that we develop.

The "NCTE Beliefs" tells us that "developing writers require support. This support can best come through carefully designed writing instruction oriented toward acquiring new strategies and skills. Certainly, writers can benefit from teachers who simply support and give them time to write. However, instruction matters." As the "NCTE Beliefs" asserts, simply providing an assignment is not enough. The process of designing an effective writing assignment must include assembling the accompanying resources and crafting the instruction that will help students engage in the activity and develop as writers.

Even the best writing assignment can fail without this support: it's a lesson I learned my first year as a teacher. I knew that writing assignments were important, and our teaching advisors had spent much time during our orientation urging us to design effective ones. I still felt fairly lost, however. I knew that I needed to learn more, so in the composition pedagogy course that I was taking, I focused on assignments and wrote my first graduate paper, "Designing Writing Assignments for a Composition Curriculum." I gathered a variety of books—pedagogical books that explained how to teach writing and textbooks that included example after example of writing assignments and response prompts. I read extensively and did my best to learn as much as I could. I thought I was ready.

I redesigned the writing assignments for the next quarter I would teach. Gone were general assignments like "Write an analytical paper on symbolism in the novel." I created much more complex prompts and instructions for students. What used to be "Write an analytical paper" became more thought provoking:

> In the novel we've read, some of the characters are given
> positive, sympathetic portrayals. Others have negative, even

villainous portrayals. Still others may begin with negative qualities and gradually become more and more positive. The author gives us details, actions, and characteristics that help us figure out who is "good" and who is "bad." It's easy to know the difference in old westerns—good guys wear white hats; bad guys wear black hats. Think about the novel. How does the author indicate which characters are positive and which are negative?

With such new and improved writing assignments, I eagerly greeted the new term. But they weren't enough.

In the language of the 2001 NAEP/National Writing Project study, the problem with this revised assignment—and all of the others—was that complicating its "content and scope" alone was not sufficient to improve students' writing. To design an effective assignment, I also needed to include "organization and development." The writing assignment needed to supply "scaffolding that supports students' writing process." My delivered curriculum needed to be more extensive and student-centered to provide the support that students needed.

Without that support, students struggled with my "improved" writing task. If anything, the struggles were worse—students were lost. They either resorted to summarizing their readings or wrote vague and general responses that didn't fit the assignment. I quickly learned that you can't improve students' writing by just asking more complicated questions. Instead, students need writing assignments that provide support for the tasks that they are to complete.

Now when I use this assignment, I give students essentially the same writing prompt, but I provide more explanation before students even begin reading the novel. First, I ask the class to brainstorm characteristics of "good" and "bad" characters from a text they are all familiar with (e.g., a movie, a sitcom or cartoon, a commercial, a book that the class had read previously). As they are reading, I ask students to track relevant details in the novel using a customized bookmark or their reading journals. Their notes include page numbers, short quotations or paraphrased descriptions, and labels that indicate what the passage demonstrates. By the time students are ready to write a more formal paper, their writing process is already under way. As a result of these changes, students are more likely to make the kinds of analytical observations that I intended.

My experience that first year taught me that "instruction matters," as the "NCTE Beliefs" says. When we design writing assignments, we have to do more than design a prompting question—much more. We need to provide students with full support as they step through the writing task if we are to help them improve as writers.

2. People learn to write by writing.

I don't remember learning to write. I remember writing. I have piles of papers, beginning with high school essays on the Globe Theater and *The War of the Worlds* radio broadcast and stretching through the multiple drafts of my M.A. thesis and the various articles and software documentation that I have written since. I have piles of journals written over the course of my adult life. I have diaries in which I tracked the angst-filled highs and lows of my adolescence. I even have a hand-illustrated copy of *The Year the Easter Bunny Forgot*, apparently from third grade, given its incredibly awkward attempt at cursive handwriting.

I don't remember how I learned to string sentences together or use semicolons. Sure, I remember some specific errors and lessons. There was that first-year composition paper that I wrote when I thought that *secular* and *religious* were synonyms. Sadly, the lesson that I learned was to avoid the word *secular* completely. Even to write this paragraph, I had to look the word up to make sure I was using it correctly. I still have no confidence whatsoever in that word. I just learned not to use the word *secular*. I didn't learn anything about writing from that experience.

There have been specific moments when I suddenly realized that I knew how to write. On a recent day, after writing dozens of ReadWriteThink lesson plans and teaching ideas for NCTE's INBOX, I realized that my writing had changed. I'm sure it changed long before I ever noticed it, but that afternoon, it seemed obvious. I had finally become comfortable with a new voice: I knew how to write from an authoritative stance. Prior to that point, I felt as if I had been trying to weave together the positions expressed by a bunch of other people, connecting all the quotations gathered from my research on composition and language arts instruction in an expository dot-to-dot drawing.

At some point, I began writing from my own position and with my own voice. I was still including quotations from my research, but I was no longer simply connecting other people's ideas. I don't know when my writing actually changed, but I know when I realized it because I recorded the moment in a blog entry that day:

> Can a writer's voice and style change in a matter of a few months, almost a year?
>
> Maybe it's not that the voice has changed, but that I've finally found it. I reread something that I wrote in June or July. It's been sitting in its folder ever since. I just haven't had the chance or the

energy to write. But I pulled it out, and I felt almost compelled to grab a pen and mark out huge sections—sections that felt like a fake attempt at sounding like I knew what I was doing. It read to me like a sort of unnatural pasting together of varying sources.

I read it, and I suddenly knew that that wasn't my voice. My voice is different now. Much more straightforward, stronger. It feels very odd, and odder still that I don't know whether my voice changed—or maybe I had it all along and I just never heard it. Whatever the answer, maybe now I can get that manuscript written.

I didn't learn this new voice and style from any teacher or classes that I was taking. It didn't even come from a book I was reading. The change just happened over time, as I wrote more and more lesson plans and teacher resources. The time that I spent doing all that writing and re-writing actually changed the way that I write.

I learned to write by writing—and that's how students in most effective writing classrooms learn to write. Writing instruction needs to focus directly on writing, not on talking about writing or reading about writing. The delivered curriculum needs to include many opportunities for students to compose. Without such opportunities, the experienced curriculum that students construct short-circuits the writing process and thus does not adequately value writing.

The "NCTE Beliefs" explains it this way: "As is the case with many other things people do, getting better at writing requires doing it—a lot. This means actual writing, not merely listening to lectures about writing, doing grammar drills, or discussing readings. The more people write, the easier it gets and the more they are motivated to do it."

For a writing assignment, this means incorporating multiple opportunities for writing and encouraging students to write frequently. A writing assignment may ask students to write a descriptive essay, an informative report, or a persuasive letter. The best writing assignments, however, do not limit writing activities to a primary task. As we design writing assignments, we need to structure such options for writing. The "NCTE Beliefs about the Teaching of Writing" suggest that "writing instruction must include ample in-class and out-of-class opportunities for writing and should include writing for a variety of purposes and audiences."

Every assignment, regardless of the audience and purpose, can include writing that is meant for a range of purposes. For a persuasive letter to the editor, for example, I ask students to jot down characteristics of example letters in the newspaper, summarize the article they will respond to, consult guiding questions when analyzing sample letters, use a graphic organizer to arrange ideas, compose rough drafts, refer to peer review questions when responding to another student's draft, and revise their own drafts.

Additionally, the writing does not have to be part of the formal structure of the assignment itself. Beyond writing specific pieces like those for the persuasive letters, for instance, I encourage students to write for themselves as they discover and explore their topics. I ask them to write directly to me about the topic, their progress, and any concerns or questions. I ask them to write to each other, writing questions for the peer readers who consider their drafts. I encourage students to add sticky note annotations to their drafts as well as to the books that they are reading. In short, I ask students to write quite often in the process of composing the final text for an assignment. By using such strategies, each writing assignment can, as the "NCTE Beliefs" suggests, "support students in the development of writing lives, habits, and preferences for life outside school."

3. Writing is a process.

When I first began teaching, I brought in folders containing my own rough drafts, notes, handwritten revisions, and final pieces. I wanted students to see what writing looked like, so I put my own writing process on display. Today, there are more electronic files and fewer pieces of paper, but I still share my notes, drafts, and various annotations.

Writing assignments must accomplish this same goal—they have to show students what the writing process looks like, and they have to encourage students to discover their own writing process. The "NCTE Beliefs" suggests specifically how we can address the writing process in the classroom: "Whenever possible, teachers should attend to the process that students might follow to produce texts—and not only specify criteria for evaluating finished products, in form or content. Students should become comfortable with pre-writing techniques, multiple strategies for developing and organizing a message, a variety of strategies for revising and editing, and strategies for preparing products for public audiences and for deadlines. In explaining assignments, teachers should provide guidance and options for ways of going about it." To support process-based writing, then, assignments need to go beyond just providing a prompt for the finished product. They need to include support and structures that encourage students to engage fully in process-based writing, and they need to provide time for students to complete multiple drafts. A fairly basic assignment might ask students to complete the following task:

> Working with group members, use descriptive language to create a restaurant menu that gives your customers enough details to make an informed decision. Your group can choose the kind of restaurant, the features to include on the menu, and the specific menu items. Each group should turn in notes, rough drafts, and revisions, along with the final copy of the menu.

By asking students to turn in all drafts and to complete specific tasks, the prompt makes a good start at providing an effective assignment.

Even better is a writing assignment that encourages students to engage in the writing activity in ways that support the development of their own individual writing processes. Students should never be forced to follow a single process, because no two writers are the same. Every writer follows a different process, and that process can change because of the writer's audience, purpose, and situation. Writing assignments, then, should provide the support that will allow students to develop and refine their own processes. Consider this revised description of the assignment students will complete:

> Working with group members, explore the genre of menus by analyzing existing menus from local restaurants. Pay attention to the words that the menus use and the ways that they have been put together to convince restaurant-goers to order the meals. After establishing the characteristics of the genre, your group will choose a restaurant and then create your own custom menus. Be sure to collect and save all the notes that you take as you explore examples so that you can return to them as you work.

In the revised assignment, students begin their writing process immediately by exploring the genre. Their research is part of the assignment and provides the structure for the first activities that they complete. At the same time, the process of gathering ideas isn't prescribed for the class. Students are given examples and encouraged to explore and make observations. The delivered curriculum makes room for the writing process in ways that allow students to develop as writers. Although structures are in place to help move them along, students are not given a step-by-step outline that would interrupt the natural development of their writing. As a result of these changes to the activity, when students begin their drafts, they have already seen a range of options for their own writing.

A strong assignment continues to provide such support throughout the writing process. By providing planning sheets, offering suggestions for exploration, and encouraging peer discussion and feedback, a writing assignment can demonstrate various aspects of the writing process. At all times, however, students need to have choices to ensure that the activity never pushes them into a forced or formulaic writing process.

4. Writing is a tool for thinking.

I love "light bulb moments"—those moments when you're working with students and you see their sudden understanding of a new idea or concept. Those are the moments I live for in the classroom—those moments when a student "gets it."

Sometimes they happen in a writing conference. They can happen in class, as students talk about their papers in small groups or with the whole class. They can be revealed in a draft or journal entry. The thing about the light bulb moments in a writing class is that they often spring in one way or another from writing.

I remember in particular William's light bulb moment. My first-year college composition class in spring 1993 focused on the ways that the writer's perspective affects the meaning and language of a message. Students read pieces by Jane Tompkins, Harriet Jacobs, and Alice Walker, and we talked about how writing takes place in a social context. I asked the class to do some fairly complex and sophisticated thinking, and their writing showed that they were struggling a bit with the task.

One day in the middle of this course, William was slow to gather his belongings and leave, so I asked him if he had a question.

He stepped up to the desk and said, "I've been watching some of the TV about that thing in Waco. You seen it?" He was referring to the ATF raid on the Branch Davidian ranch near Waco, Texas, and the subsequent siege that was still under way there.

"I was writing about it in my journal," he continued. "You see different reports and stuff on different channels." I nodded, and he went on: "When they talk to the witnesses, they say different things about it and it has to do with what they care about. That's just like those things we've been reading. That's what you're talking about, right?"

A light bulb moment! He didn't know it, but William had had a light bulb moment as he wrote that journal entry and made the connections between what he had been reading and current events.

Many people believe that such ideas spring forth fully formed when people write, but writing teachers know that people frequently find and develop ideas *as they write*. When we ask students to freewrite, brainstorm, complete graphic organizers, or compose drafts, we are asking them to use writing as a tool for thinking—to discover, explore, and develop their ideas as they write. This time for thinking and exploring is perhaps the hardest piece of the delivered curriculum for students to recognize in their construction of the experienced curriculum.

The "NCTE Beliefs" explains that "in any writing classroom, some of the writing is for others and some of the writing is for the writer. Regardless of the age, ability, or experience of the writer, the use of writing to generate thought is still valuable; therefore, forms of writing such as personal narrative, journals, written reflections, observations, and writing-to-learn strategies are important."

In William's case, journal writing led him to make connections among the texts that he was reading and viewing. As we design writing assignments, we need to make room for such writing-to-learn components. Journals are a good start, but the assignments that we design can provide a range of explicit opportunities to use writing as a tool for thinking. "In any writing assignment," the "NCTE Beliefs" tells us, "it must be assumed that part of the work of writers will involve generating and regenerating ideas prior to writing them." In fact, asking students to reflect on their writing frequently makes them better aware of the writing habits and knowledge that they construct as they complete the assignments for a course.

Even a simple narrative assignment can demonstrate how this kind of writing and thinking can intertwine. Simply share a picture that tells a story and then encourage students to brainstorm words and ideas about the image before they write a story that gives background on the image or extends the story it tells. As they work on this task, students have the chance to think critically about their interpretations of the events in the image and to write about those ideas by brainstorming and freewriting. As they do this writing, they are analyzing the image and synthesizing the information that they find there. They are using writing as a tool for thinking. When they begin to shape their ideas into these detailed narratives, students have already been "generating and regenerating ideas prior to writing them" in their more formal papers.

5. Writing grows out of many different purposes.

"But I got As last year, and now you're telling me this is a D?"

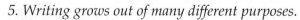

How many times have I heard that question in writing conferences with students, and rarely could I help but feel sorry for these students, who usually pleaded later in our conversation, "But what do you want?"

The frustration students expressed in these conferences was probably not their fault—or, at worst, was their fault only because they have spent their time in the classroom attempting to do whatever they believed teachers wanted. The "NCTE Beliefs" explains: "Often, in school, students write only to prove that they did something they were asked to do, in order to get credit for it. Or, students are taught a single type of writing and are led to believe this type will suffice in all situations."

When students write to prove what they know, whether it's specific content or a writing form, they *are* paying attention to audience and purpose as they actively construct the experienced curriculum of the class. With all the materials and social situations that students analyze in the classroom, their ultimate goal is simply to construct a curriculum that will give them the best grade. For them, that boils down to a basic issue: What does the teacher want? Students unconsciously know that rhetorical needs drive the writing that they do when they pursue the answer to this question. They know, as the "NCTE Beliefs" states, that "writing grows out of many different purposes." The email message that a student sends her two fathers saying that her favorite band is coming to town is different from the text message that same student sends to her best friends about the concert. The general information in the messages may be the same, but the language and the details of the two pieces of writing will probably be quite different.

In many academic writing situations, students demonstrate that they believe that the purpose is to get a good grade and the audience is the teacher. Those choices, although understandable, may not align with the purpose and audience that the teacher intended for the writing assignment. When students beg me to tell them what I want, they are showing that they understand how much audience shapes writing. They know that I am the reader who will grade their papers, so they want to know what I'll be looking for when I read them. They are trying to achieve the purpose, as they see it, for the writing assignment.

To move students beyond this simplistic analysis of their writing situations, assignments need to focus on authentic communication and on a range of different kinds of writing for different audiences. In many classes, the basic kind of writing is determined by someone other than the student, who may be asked to compose an informative essay, a business letter, or an audio narrative. Because the purpose of the writing is typically determined for them by the teacher, and not by their own needs for communication, students often have no purpose for their writing beyond pleasing the teacher in order to receive a good grade.

This predicament is addressed in the "NCTE Beliefs" directly: "Writers outside of school have many different purposes beyond demonstrating accountability, and they practice myriad types and genres. In order to make sure students are learning how writing differs when the purpose and the audience differ, it is important that teachers create opportunities for students to be in different kinds of writing situations, where the relationships and agendas are varied."

Because they take these facts into account, the best writing assignments are interconnected and complex documents that invite students to create more than one kind of writing for more than one audience. Although a basic assignment can require that students write only drafts of an essay, a more effective assignment asks for a range of artifacts and audiences:

- journal writing to explore the topic
- an email message proposing the essay topic to the teacher
- a bulletin board message explaining the essay topic to a writing group
- a response on a bulletin board to peers' topics
- essay drafts, some read by group members or the teacher
- comments to peer reviewers (questions about the current draft, etc.)
- peer review feedback to classmates
- a final draft reflections letter to the teacher

This collection of artifacts addresses multiple purposes and three or more audiences (classmates, teacher, and writer)—and all that without any attention to the audiences and purposes for the essay itself.

Further, the artifacts produced in response to an effective writing assignment differ from other composing that students have recently completed. Each writing assignment should be part of a larger curriculum that focuses on writing for a range of different audiences and purposes. In other words, designing effective writing assignments involves attention to the assignments that have come before and those that will come after. The entire series of writing assignments matters. Looking across the range of assignments, you should see different audiences and purposes. Naturally, assignments should not be arranged randomly—there should be connections among the activities as well. These examples show the range of purposes and audiences that a series might include, while also suggesting a thematic connection among the activities:

- a personal reflection on why a local place is important to the writer, to be shared with classmates
- a description of a memorable local place or a narrative that tells the story of a day in the place, written for someone who has never been there, perhaps in the form of a brochure for the local library
- a process essay that explains how to do something that takes place there, for someone who doesn't know how to do the thing
- a classification that outlines the ways that the local place is used by others, written to convince others to visit the location
- a letter to the editor that urges the public to take some action or position in relation to the local place (for instance, continued funding for a local park)

Notice that even in these brief assignment suggestions, the purpose and audience for the writing are clear. Inclusion of those details is the most basic element of an effective writing assignment. If we are to move students beyond thinking that all their writing in a course is simply for the teacher to grade, all in pursuit of a good final grade, we have to design assignments that make the purpose and audience for the writing precise and clear. We have to be explicit with students about what we really want: effective writing that pays attention to the audience and purpose we intend for the activity.

6. Conventions of finished and edited texts are important to readers and therefore to writers.

When I meet new people online, I hide my profession as long as possible to avoid seeing the comment "Oh, no, better watch my spelling!" in the chat window. Who among us hasn't confessed she was an English teacher and been greeted by such anxious responses? For a great many people, mention English teachers, and you bring up nightmares of grammar rules, spelling words, and incomprehensible punctuation marks.

I really don't sit around marking up every text with a red pen. While it's true that I understand the mysteries of the semicolon, I'm more likely to care about what something says than whether the words and punctuation are just right. Okay, I'll admit that I do chuckle when I see an advertisement for an upcoming "Clarence Sale" or a church bulletin announcement that reveals "The choir will sin at both services." But in such cases, those of us with practice in reading the English language still know what the text is meant to say: we can see past the error to the actual intention. Readers still learning the English language, however, may be confused.

The difference between what a text says and what it means is a crucial one. When errors of spelling, punctuation, or grammar affect what a text actually says, the writer's purpose may not be accomplished. English teachers know this, but students often do not understand this concept. Further, when students do not fully understand the conventions in question, they can't see why their meaning is unclear. The challenge for teachers is balancing these issues of correctness with issues of content development and expression. As the "NCTE Beliefs" explains, "every teacher has to resolve a tension between writing as generating and shaping ideas and writing as demonstrating expected surface conventions. On the one hand, it is important for writing to be as correct as possible and for students to be able to produce correct texts. On the other hand, achieving correctness is only one set of things writers must be able to do; a correct text empty of ideas or unsuited to its audience or purpose is not a good piece of writing." Effective writing assignments address this tension by providing structures and support that focus on conventions without abandoning other aspects of writing. Simply telling students to attend to the conventions of spelling, punctuation, and grammar isn't enough. Students need to have details on what to look for and explanations of how to search for it embedded in the delivered assignment.

As I design writing assignments, I include structures that encourage attention to the conventional issues of writing. The timing of this support is crucial to its effectiveness however. I never ask students to focus on conventions early in the process and never to the exclusion of other writing issues. If issues of grammar, punctuation, and mechanics are raised too early, they can circumvent the writing processes and its development by shifting attention away from exploring and focusing on the message. Despite the significance of timing in providing support, dealing with conventions in the writing assignment itself can be relatively simple. When I create the schedule for a writing project, I ask for drafts at several points to encourage a fully developed writing process. As I review later drafts, I sketch out time to review grammar and punctuation, and I remind students to take time for spellchecking.

Scheduling support in this way ensures a basic level of attention to grammar, but students also need writing assignments to include information on specific conventions that are important to the assignment.

The "NCTE Beliefs" states, "Writers need an image in their minds of conventional grammar, spelling, and punctuation in order to compare what is already on the page to an ideal of correctness. They also need to be aware of stylistic options that will produce the most desirable impression on their readers. All of the dimensions of editing are motivated by a concern for an audience."

In practice, this guideline means that attention to conventions has to be integrated in ways that flow with each writer's process and has to be designed in ways that make connections to the writer's purpose and audience clear. Say I'm designing a literary analysis assignment that asks students to explore the purpose and effectiveness of a specific symbol from a reading. In addition to talking about the literary element of symbolism and the other characteristics of the literary text, this writing assignment needs to talk about how conventions relating to quotations from the text will be important to meaning in students' papers. After students have spent time identifying symbols and supporting evidence for their interpretations, I'd schedule class time to talk about how to format and punctuate the quotations they'll use as evidence in their papers—*and* I'd schedule time for students to review their drafts for these issues. An effective writing assignment, in other words, not only asks students to pay attention to correct expression; it also allows time to talk about correct expression and answer questions that students have about the rules and guidelines for the texts that they are writing.

7. Writing and reading are related.

Before I figured out how to compose effective writing assignments, I knew the powerful connection between reading and writing—although, to be honest, I didn't realize the important underlying connections between the practices that I had adopted. Early on, I found that when I provided students with models and talked about how those models worked, students wrote more effective essays. My favorite textbooks for writing classes were those that included student essays, which we discussed in detail in class. Naturally, I collected my own student examples over time and added them to the resources from the texts to use for group discussions.

Why was this practice so effective? As the "NCTE Beliefs" explains, "in order to write a particular kind of text, it helps if the writer has read that kind of text. In order to take on a particular style of language, the writer needs to have read that language, to have heard it in her mind, so that she can hear it again in order to compose it." By sharing published and student essays, I intuitively recognized the facts behind this belief: "Writing and reading are related. People who read a lot have a much easier time getting better at writing."

Whether they are used as background resources or as models for student writing, effective writing assignments should include readings. At times, those readings can provide the framing model for students' own writing. Nonfiction picture books, for instance, can provide structures that students can use as they complete research projects. In other circumstances, students might compose their own versions of a text that they have read, adapting the original published text to a new situation or topic. Parodies, for example, provide a great way for students to explore and analyze texts. Model readings need not be published texts, however. Student essays are also a vital resource when designing writing assignments. Some textbooks include these essays, but to add to my collection, I always ask students for permission to make copies of their texts for use with future students.

Simply providing these models is only the beginning, of course. Modeling is just as important as models: to help students learn strategies for developing the deeper reading and more sophisticated analysis that lead to stronger writing, the delivered curriculum must show them how people read and write essays. One of my most successful class sessions focused on a deep reading of song lyrics. Students were writing explications of a song of their choice (which I had approved, of course). I brought in the lyrics to "Old Friends/Bookends" by Paul Simon and Art Garfunkel, an older song that students were unlikely to choose as the focus for their own papers.

I passed out copies of the lyrics, played the song for the class, and then went through the lyrics carefully, line-by-line and word-by-word, demonstrating how I explicate a text. Students became involved in the discussion and added their own comments, observations, and connections to the lyrics. We covered the chalkboards with notes until we ran out of space. Reading the lyrics went beyond simply reading the text out loud. Reading, in this instance, involved modeling how to read a text.

With all this information gathered, together we created some possible outlines and key sentences for essays on the students' songs. When they left the class, the students had seen and participated in a deep reading activity that provided models for their own work. They had seen the connections between reading and writing in practice. To provide students with the support they need to do their best work, effective writing assignments develop these relationships as a natural part of the activity. Assignments do not always lend themselves to the kind of deep reading that I was able to demonstrate with the Simon and

Garfunkel lyrics, but there are always links between reading and writing, and effective assignments highlight and build on those connections.

8. Writing has a complex relationship to talk.

I talk about writing all the time—probably too much, if you ask my family. I can't help it. I spend a lot of time writing, and it's what I know best, so it's what I talk about. But I don't talk about writing simply because it's what I do. There have been numerous times when I worked out what I wanted to write by talking about the text with friends, family, and colleagues. There have been many important conversations that I first had on paper, writing down what I wanted to communicate before I spoke to the person involved. It's widely accepted that public speakers create notes before they present, but I've been known to even write notes before calling a company on the phone to talk about a billing problem or ask for customer support with a new piece of software or hardware. My handwritten notes are fundamentally important when I go to visit my doctor. Without writing out everything that I want to say to her, I'm not sure that I would ever remember to discuss all of the important aspects of my health care. In other words, I talk about writing and I write about talking because I know that it makes my communication stronger.

The "NCTE Beliefs" describes how these connections between writing and talking affect teaching: "As they grow, writers still need opportunities to talk about what they are writing about, to rehearse the language of their upcoming texts and run ideas by trusted colleagues before taking the risk of committing words to paper. After making a draft, it is often helpful for writers to discuss with peers what they have done, partly in order to get ideas from their peers, partly to see what they, the writers, say when they try to explain their thinking. Writing conferences, wherein student writers talk about their work with a teacher, who can make suggestions or re-orient what the writer is doing, are also very helpful uses of talk in the writing process."

Effective writing assignments include such relationships. If we ask students to think carefully, they find that they also have strong connections between their writing and their talking, but the challenge is that they may not recognize those connections themselves. I like to arrange assignments so that they include time for conferences early in the writing process. I ask students to talk to me about the writing they've done so far and, as they speak, I jot down what they say. When I ask them to then point out any places in their writing where they need help, I refer back to the notes that I've written. Typically, the challenge is easily addressed by reminding them of something that they mentioned in our discussion but students simply haven't yet connected what they know and talked about with what they have written in the text. In other words, in their experienced curriculum, they haven't constructed the connections between what they already know and what they are trying to accomplish.

In addition to peer discussion and writing conferences, oral description and drafting can prove to be useful prewriting techniques that get writers started on their drafts quickly. Narrative writing lends itself well to such a prewriting strategy because students are great natural oral storytellers. Simply ask students to tell their stories to one another in small groups before they begin drafting. Group members can take notes on the storyteller's tale, passing all of the notes along after the tale is told. When writing assignments are designed to include such activities, students' talk becomes a key strategy in their writing.

9. Literate practices are embedded in complicated social relationships.

All students are language experts. The lived curriculum that they bring to the classroom is wide-ranging: They know and have used language extensively before they come to the classroom. They may be struggling with academic language, content-area language, or even the English language itself—the delivered curriculum for their classes—but they have extensive and sophisticated language abilities. They are readers and writers. They communicate with friends, family, teachers, co-workers, classmates, and neighbors.

The "NCTE Beliefs" explains that "writing happens in the midst of a web of relationships." This social web extends beyond writing to all communicative acts that students take. Reading a *Halo 3* cheat website, composing a Facebook profile, instant messaging with friends, speaking to the family around the kitchen table—all these literacy acts demonstrate students' understanding of sophisticated social relationships.

Students are clearly highly skilled language users, just not necessarily users of the kind of language that is expected for success in the classroom. Further, every student has different language experiences. Even if a group of students had the same language arts teacher, the members of that group would have varied personal language backgrounds that influenced their interactions with that teacher—and they would have extensive language experiences that had taken place outside that teacher's classroom. Every writer has a different social web that influences his or her literacy practices.

So many educators have mentioned that the "one size fits all" notion does not apply to teaching. In the case of language experiences, the adage is especially apt. As the "NCTE Beliefs" explains, "writers start in different places. It makes a difference what kind of language a writer spoke while growing up, and what kinds of language they are being asked to take on later in their experience. It makes a difference, too, the culture a writer comes from, the ways people use language in that culture and the degree to which that culture is privileged in the larger society. Important cultural differences are not only ethnic but also racial, economic, geographical and ideological."

With the complicated patchwork of experiences that students bring to the classroom, it seems impossible for one activity to meet the needs of every student. Nonetheless, teachers must find assignments that can support writers who all begin at different starting places. A well-designed writing assignment can accomplish this goal, but it's important to understand the difference between focusing the content of an assignment on different ways of using language and including support for students with a range of language experiences. I used the following assignment when I first began teaching, but now I realize that it fails to provide that kind of support:

> Write a paper that traces the influence of a particular movie, song, book, person, or television show upon language use. Were there words or phrases related to the source you've chosen that were adopted by the general public? Who adopted them? How were they used? How long lasting was their influence? Why do you think they were adopted while words and phrases from other sources weren't? And perhaps most important, what can you conclude about the ways that language use is influenced?

The problem with my old assignment is that although the content focuses on recognizing students as language experts, it does not provide the supporting resources that would help students with different backgrounds write as well as they can. The writing assignment talks about language knowledge in a general way. Language is the content only. The assignment doesn't provide any way for students' experiences to fit into their exploration of the issue. More problematically, the prompt does not provide scaffolding for students with different backgrounds, nor does it highlight the language requirements for the activity.

Compare that old prompt with the Pop Culture Dictionary Assignment in Figure 2.1, which also focuses on pop culture's influence on language but provides more support for students. From the first sentence, my new assignment encourages greater awareness of the social web of language that students bring to the classroom. The focus of the assignment is not a general discussion of culture's influence on language but a specific discussion of one cultural influence on students' own language.

Of course, every writing assignment cannot focus on the topic of language; we have to develop other ways that an effective writing assignment supports students' language knowledge. In the revised assignment, notice that students write in at least three different kinds of language: the academic language of dictionaries, the language of the popular culture text, and one of their own (likely more informal) languages.

For this particular assignment, the different varieties of language or dialect are included in the final artifact, but that need not be the case for an assignment to lead to effective writing. Students can write in an informal or home language in their journals as they begin prewriting, they can quote the languages of others in their research, they can use semiformal English in peer review with classmates, and they can use the academic language of the classroom in their final drafts. Since knowledge in one language transfers to another language, the inclusion in all assignments of opportunities for students to demonstrate their language abilities makes these assignments more effective and shows students that we value their range of language knowledge.

10. Composing occurs in different modalities and technologies.

Digital technologies have revolutionized much of the way that I write. I make starts and stops constantly as I draft. I try changes that I know I can easily undo without losing the original text. I can play around with white space, paragraphing, and headings until I get the best design.

In the past, writing was sometimes a one-shot deal involving erasable typing paper, Wite-Out, a very slow pace, and a lot of hoping. Often I composed complicated rough drafts with arrows, highlighted text, and many notes, but once I started typing, I was stuck. There was no way to change things without starting all over, so I learned to live with that first shot at a full draft.

Now I move passages around regularly, and I focus far more attention on the nonalphabetic aspects of my writing. If an illustration would help my point, I can easily add it to what I'm writing and get a polished result. When I share my draft with others, they can use software to comment on the exact passages they want to suggest changes

Pop Culture Dictionary Assignment

Choose a particular pop culture text that has influenced your use of language. You might choose a movie, song, music video, book, celebrity, political movement, television show, or website.

Create five dictionary entries that define and provide details on words from the pop culture text. Your five words should be from one text or related texts. Any of the following would be acceptable choices:

- five phrases from a single television show but not necessarily all from the same episode
- five words used by a particular celebrity
- five words or phrases used in a series of movies (like the Harry Potter movies)
- five phrases used in a recent horror film
- five words used by a band in its latest videos

Each entry should include the word, its definition, an example of its use from the original pop culture text, an example of how you use the word in conversation, and basic etymology (the origin of the word's meaning).

Along with your entries, write a short introduction that explains what the original pop culture text is, who has been influenced by it, and how the words are most often used (e.g., in casual conversation with others who watch the television show). Your introduction can also discuss how widespread the influence of the text has been on language and predict how long the influence will last.

Figure 2.1. This revised assignment focuses on a single pop culture influence on students' own language.

for, thereby giving me more specific feedback than I ever got from peer readers when I was a student.

In the years that have passed since I first composed on a computer keyboard in 1980, I have come to truly understand the significance of the assertion in the "NCTE Beliefs" that as writers compose in different modalities and technologies, "'writing' comes to mean more than scratching words with pen and paper." Writing is placing words on screens and paper, recording words and sounds and images on video, arranging words and images and sounds in audio and video recordings, and creating links between all these means of expression.

Students still compose old-fashioned printouts and handwritten documents, but they can and do compose in many more formats—PowerPoint and KeyNote presentations, blogs, Web pages, email messages, audio recordings, videos, photographs, still images, oral presentations, text messages, spreadsheets, animations, hypertexts, podcasts. This constantly evolving list goes far beyond "scratching words with pen and paper," and, as a result, effective writing assignments must similarly extend the tasks that students are asked to complete. The "NCTE Beliefs" presents this goal directly:

> Writing instruction must accommodate the explosion in technology from the world around us.
>
> From the use of basic word processing to support drafting, revision, and editing to the use of hypertext and the infusion of visual components in writing, the definition of what writing instruction includes must evolve to embrace new requirements.

As we design writing assignments, then, we must recognize the roles that various modalities play in students' composing repertoire. For example, prewriting work can include drawings, conversations, written or typed notes, audio notes, scanned texts, and more. As part of a description of a place, students might take photos, film videos, or record the sounds of the place as part of their prewriting. Those various artifacts might become part of the description later or simply be inspiration and idea gathering for the final descriptive text.

Effective writing assignments allow for and even encourage such a range of composing opportunities for students, a range that supports the multiple intelligences that students bring to the classroom. Rather than propose a traditional analytical paper on *Romeo and Juliet*, for instance, an assignment might ask students to compose a PowerPoint or KeyNote presentation that communicates the same messages as a soliloquy in the play. Such an option allows students to use text, sounds, animations, film clips, and images in their work.

The problem with such an assignment, however, is that students without adequate technology access outside of the classroom are at a distinct disadvantage. In addition to allowing for a range of composing modalities, we must also pay attention to the composing tools available to students. The "NCTE Beliefs" reminds us that "many teachers and students do not, however, have adequate access to computing, recording, and video equipment to take advantage of the most up-to-date technologies. In many cases, teaching about the multi-modal nature of writing is best accomplished through varying the forms of writing with more ordinary implements." Providing students with a range of options that includes "more ordinary implements" leads to stronger and more effective assignments. Further, by giving students the opportunity to choose the modality that best fits their abilities, a range of options also gives students the chance to choose the alternative that will lead to their best work.

Instead of asking every student to create a PowerPoint presentation on *Romeo and Juliet,* a more effective writing assignment, as shown in Modern-Day Interpretation Projects in Figure 2.2, provides a range of possible writing tasks that students can compose using whatever technology is available. Students without access to technology can write print-based newspaper articles. Instant messages, blog entries, and scripts can all be written with paper and pen. By providing options that let students choose the modality and tools in this way, effective writing assignments not only show an awareness of the wide range of ways that people compose but also provide support for the many ways of thinking and composing that students bring to the classroom.

11. Assessment of writing involves complex, informed, human judgment.

"I got a Godzilla!" one of my students bragged from the back of the classroom. And with that exclamation, one of the most successful grading techniques I've ever used was under way.

It really all began as a sort of joke. I was using a behavioral grading method, as described in Glenn J. Broadhead and Richard C. Freed's *The Variables of Composition: Process and Product in a Business Setting,* to teach business writing. I assigned only pass/fail grades to the work, and students had to compile a certain number of passes to get various grades. I had read an article arguing that in the business world you don't get As and Bs: you either get a pass and send the piece out or get told to redo the work. Pedagogically, the system was attractive because it allowed students to learn from their work on the various drafts, rather than punishing them for every misstep.

Modern-Day Interpretation Projects

1. Headline News Story. Choose a modern-day event that mirrors an event that occurred in the text. Create a headline news Web page and two or three related links based on the event for a Web-based news site. To get an idea of length, format, and the kinds of links typically included in such stories, visit news sites on the Web.

2. Instant Messages or Text Messages. Rewrite a dialogue between two characters from the text in modern-day format as if it took place online through instant messages or on cell phones or another tool using text messages.

3. Blog. Rewrite a monologue from the text (e.g., the speech of one person) as a blog entry or a series of blog entries. Include appropriate links to other Web pages and comments that other characters from the text might leave on the blog entries.

4. Podcast. Rewrite a monologue or dialogue from the text as a podcast (a self-published syndicated "radio show"). Record your project as an audio file or create the transcript of the show that you might post online with the audio file. Be sure to include details on background sounds and music if you write a transcript.

5. What If? Find a scene in the text that you believe would have been radically different given the existence of a certain piece of advanced high-tech equipment. Name the item and describe how and why the scene would have been different and how it would have affected the outcome of the play.

6. Digital Artifacts. Imagine that you find a portable disk next to the computer of one of the characters from the text. It might be a floppy disk, Zip disk, USB keychain disk, or another device. This storage disk contains personal documents—letters, "to do" lists, data, and poems written by the character for his or her eyes only. Decide on four or five documents, recreate them, invent file names for each, and create a (fake) printout of the disk directory. Put all these together in a packet about the character.

7. Playlist. Choose one of the characters from the text and create a playlist that that character would have on his or her iPod or MP3 player. Invent the name for the playlist and create a list of the names of the songs, the artists, the albums the songs came from, and other relevant details in your word processor. Alternately, if you have the resources available, you can burn a CD of the character's playlist and create a CD label with the appropriate details.

8. Reality TV Show. Imagine that the characters from the text are part of a reality TV show. Rewrite a scene from the text as it would have been caught from the surveillance cameras of the show. Film your scene using a video camera or write a transcript of it (including details on background sounds, setting, and props).

9. Technology Product Endorsement. Have a character in the text endorse a technology product—design a letter or short narrative in which the character tells readers why they should purchase or support the product.

10. PowerPoint Presentation. Rewrite a monologue from the text as a PowerPoint presentation. Imagine that the character is presenting the information to a modern audience using, images, and other features available in PowerPoint (or another computer-based presentation tool).Create the PowerPoint presentation that the character would use.

Figure 2.2. This range of tasks gives students options for using technology.

Providing feedback in this system was a little challenging though. The article had suggested using checkmarks on students' work. It's not that I usually mistrust students, but I realized that it would be easy for an unethical student to fake a checkmark or other such handwritten mark on a paper. My solution was to use some stamps and an ink pad to indicate the pass or fail mark on the paper. As part of my explanation of the system to the class, I showed them the stamp that I would use on their passing work: a fairly generic red happy face stamp that I'd picked up at the office supply store. I didn't add any special mark to students' work that did not meet the requirements. Instead, unless the paper had been marked with the specified red happy face, it wasn't acceptable.

Simply because I had a red Godzilla stamp with me when I was describing the system, I told students that if they made sloppy mistakes, such as failing to spellcheck, they'd get the Godzilla stamped on their papers. I really intended that to be the end of it, but over the first days of the course, students were curious about the mysterious Godzilla stamp. Some students had even taken to pointing out errors that they thought were probably worthy of the Godzilla, but they explained, "She's just being nice" as they compared drafts and worked on peer review together.

Finally, I gave in. One evening as I was grading, I ran across a basic error in the paper of one student who had been particularly insistent in questioning when the Godzilla would appear. I stamped his paper with the Godzilla, went on to the next one, and didn't think anything of it until his enthusiastic response in class that next morning.

In short time, the Godzilla stamp became the highlight of each class. When I returned papers, students eagerly searched out the Godzillas and discussed in their writing groups what they'd gotten wrong in the editing process. In conferences with me, students would pull out Godzilla-stamped texts and explain their errors to me in the course of discussing other, deeper issues related to their work. When someone who frequently found Godzillas on every paper got a Godzilla-free paper, there was much pride—not just from the writer but from the entire writing group. It was the one and only time in my teaching career that giving negative feedback was taken as positive support rather than as criticism. I'm not sure I could ever repeat the way that that particular class embraced the Godzilla stamp, but it was fun while it lasted.

The reaction to that stamp helped teach me the importance of formative feedback. When students are actively involved in ongoing assessment, during peer review and in writing groups as well as in student-teacher conferences, assessment criteria become more concrete for them. Prior to that course, the feedback that I gave students included commenting on rough drafts and discussing work in student-teacher conferences, but never before had I spent so much time on ongoing feedback as students were in the process of writing. During all of this feedback and interaction, the students and I constructed an experienced curriculum in which error was okay because it was a legitimate learning experience. Students could make errors without negative consequences and with the understanding that they would have the chance to improve their work. It was a labor-intensive course for me, but it was clear that when students had more continuing feedback, they worked together as members of writing groups more successfully and they wrote more effectively.

The "NCTE Beliefs" identifies two kinds of assessment that teachers of writing should use with writers: "Instructors must recognize the difference between formative and summative evaluation and be prepared to evaluate students' writing from both perspectives. By formative evaluation here, we mean provisional, ongoing, in-process judgments about what students know and what to teach next. By summative evaluation, we mean final judgments about the quality of student work. Teachers of writing must also be able to recognize the developmental aspects of writing ability and devise appropriate lessons for students at all levels of expertise." Effective writing assignments include details on the feedback students will receive: both on the ongoing feedback that will be available and on the final criteria used to judge the finished piece. The assignments I gave students in that business writing class included both aspects. Students had summative assessment criteria for their work in the form of specific checklists of the requirements and expectations for each kind of writing that they were to complete. They also had a written description of the behavioral grading system that described the formative assessment they would receive on every piece of writing they wrote for the class. By including these assessment materials, effective writing assignments engage students in the assessment process. Students know what the criteria are for their work and are better able to work toward fulfilling them.

In addition to formative and summative assessment, effective writing assignments include opportunities for self-assessment and reflection for students. The "NCTE Beliefs" asserts that such reflection activities "contribute to a writer's development and ability to move among genres, media, and rhetorical situations." I typically use draft letters to the teacher to identify students' intentions and the questions they have about the drafts they are turning in. I ask students to include comments on the parts of their work that they are satisfied with, those that they are still working on, and those that they need help with. Their comments help me focus the feedback I provide so that I address the issues that students are most concerned about. Whether I'm commenting on an early draft or a final version of students' work, these draft letters are a valuable part of the assessment process because they communicate students' understandings about the work as well as their recognition of which parts of the assignment they have completed successfully and which they believe could be improved.

How Beliefs Shape Practice

If I've written an effective writing assignment, I know that it includes all eleven of the beliefs covered in this chapter. Indeed, one thing that makes an assignment effective is the way that these pedagogical beliefs shape the design of the prompt, activities, and resources that combine to create the assignment. As I compose a writing assignment, these pedagogical beliefs influence the activities and focus of the project, the supporting resources I include, and how I schedule the different activities that students complete as they work on it.

Once we understand these underlying pedagogical beliefs and how they affect students' success as writers, the task of designing an effective writing assignment becomes easier. In an effective assignment, decisions about logistics, form, style, and content all depend upon these beliefs and how they apply to the students we teach. When we begin to design a writing assignment, we each may follow a different composing process; if we want to design an effective writing assignment, we always rely on what we know about how people learn to write.

3 Designing Writing Assignments

For me, perhaps the hardest thing about designing assignments is to remember that I am writing about writing. Frequently it seems like my attention should be on what I want students to compose—research papers, persuasive letters, description, and so forth. It's easy to dive into details on things such as the length required, the kind of documentation to be used, or the various due dates involved. But that's the wrong focus.

I need to start with the basic questions any writer considers at the beginning of a writing project: What are my goals in this piece? and Who is my audience? The details of the assignment depend upon my audience—the students I teach—rather than the end product I want them to compose. To design an effective assignment, I need to begin with *my* rhetorical situation and allow that information to shape the rhetorical situation I frame for students.

If the students are struggling writers, they'll have different needs than honors, AP, and on-level writers have—even if all of these students are generally expected to do the same kind of writing. My goal is to provide whatever group of students I am teaching with the customized information and support that they need to do their best work.

> **Three Goals for a Writing Assignment**
> Define the writing task
> Explore the expectations
> Provide supporting materials and activities

Fortunately, I can make some generalizations. Regardless of the specific audience or writing task, I need to design a collection of resources that achieves three goals: define the writing task, explore the expectations for that task, and provide supporting materials and activities. The particular details change from one group of students and writing activity to the next, but the overarching design always includes all three kinds of information.

General Writing Assignment Design

Defining the Task

Most of us begin the process of creating a writing assignment by decid-
ing what task students will complete. Research on the characteristics of
effective writing assignments tells us that as we define this task, we must
strive to do the following:

- identify an authentic audience and purpose for the project
- position students as experts in their communication with that
  audience
- ask students to interact with (rather than restate) texts and
  knowledge
- give students choices in their work that support their ownership of the task

As I define a task for a group of students, I weave together information
and options that will provide them with the raw materials they need. I
try to go beyond simply describing the end product of the assignment
and instead suggest steps in the process that students can complete,
indicate different ways that students can work, and schedule multiple
opportunities for students to write as they complete the assignment.

Exploring the Expectations for the Task

The difference between what a teacher says (or believes she has said)
and what a student hears can be the difference between success and
failure for a writing assignment. That's why an assignment sheet alone
is never enough. To ensure that students comprehend the expectations
for a writing assignment, we must also do the following:

- unpack the meaning of the assignment, as described by Jim
  Burke, by explaining the assignment to create a shared understanding of the activity
- provide model responses and demonstrate how to read and
  compose example texts
- share rubrics, checklists, and other resources that highlight the
  requirements and goals for the assignment

When I design an assignment, I prepare related models, checklists, and
rubrics, and I structure students' work so that I can check their understanding at various points in the project. When I present the assignment
to the class, I discuss both the task and the related expectations. Assessment starts at this early point, when we discuss the expectations as a
class.

Providing Support and Explanatory Materials

Although the task and the ultimate expectations may be clear, students still need support to do their best work. An effective writing assignment provides additional resources that support and engage students throughout their writing processes. Designing an assignment involves creating and gathering an entire collection of resources:

- organizational structures and material that scaffold the writing process
- multiple opportunities to write for different purposes and audiences
- writing to gather and think through ideas
- resources that address the standard conventions of finished and edited texts
- opportunities and support for peer reading and discussion as well as student-teacher conferencing

As I create an assignment sheet, I refer students to the additional supporting resources that they can consult in the process of working on the task. For example, I point to people and other texts that can offer guidance. I might include specific details from different artifacts that students will share with me and with one another during the schedule for that assignment. I will also mention additional handouts and resources that will be available at later stages in the assignment, such as graphic organizers and peer editing sheets.

With such a broad range of materials in play, it can seem as if I am moving from designing a writing assignment to creating a unit or lesson plan. When I begin to feel overwhelmed, I remind myself that this information and support is all part of the task itself. I'm not assigning an end product that appears miraculously, but an activity that calls for thinking and exploring and that also includes a written text of some kind.

Putting It All Together

No two teachers create assignments in the same way. That's really no surprise since we know that no two writers ever follow exactly the same process. Sometimes I work through the process in order: define the task, write the materials to explain the expectations, and create additional supporting resources. In other instances, I create supporting materials as a way to help define the task. Having different students and different goals usually means that the order shuffles as well. The information that students need may change while they are working on the assignment. In response, I might develop additional models, graphic organizers, or other resources.

Designing a writing assignment is rarely a one-two-three process for me. More often than not, the three tasks overlap as I work on multiple aspects of the assignment at the same time. The assignment sheet that I write probably includes information that touches on all three general goals. As I create a graphic organizer to support the assignment, I may find myself defining the task in more detail at the same time. The important thing isn't how I put the information all together but that I assemble a collection of resources that will enable students to do their best work.

To demonstrate this technique, I'll use three vignettes to work through the thought process behind the design of three different writing assignments: an inquiry assignment, an expressive writing assignment, and a persuasive writing assignment. Each of these sketches uses first-person description of the thought process that led me to a decision about a writing assignment for a specific group of students. The style is similar to a think-aloud strategy in the way that it reveals the decisions behind the assignments that I planned.

As you read, notice that all three vignettes include details that define the task, explore the expectations, and provide supporting materials, but the way in which the goals are met is fluid and organic. Each consideration affects the design in different ways, depending upon the students, the kind of writing expected, and the specific goals of the assignment.

Designing an Inquiry Assignment

It's time for the class to complete an inquiry project to meet the curriculum requirements that call for conducting research and for learning to use a variety of computer-based and print-based resources to inform a writing task. These students have written research papers in the past and have demonstrated their ability to complete a basic inquiry. They're ready for a challenge, but I need to be sure that the assignment creates a situation that will engage them and improve their research abilities.

Telling these students to write a traditional research paper about something that interests them isn't going work. All I have to do is utter the words "traditional research paper" out loud and all the wrong ideas about the assignment will spring into their heads. I want them to go beyond the standard reiteration of facts that they gather. I could focus the assignment by choosing topic areas for the class that I hope will push them into critical thinking and reflection, but making those choices may not be effective either. Instead, the topics I choose may limit students' ability to speak as experts—especially if I fall back on traditional topics such as famous historical figures or events, literary authors and periods, or controversial political or current events. From such topics, some students will find a focus that fits, but that assignment will not universally provide the best options.

I want to encourage ownership of the project by giving students more choice in what they write about. To position students as experts, I want them to choose a topic that they already consider themselves authorities on. Anything from soccer to NASCAR and video games to outdoor grilling will work. If students know about famous figures and events, those will make fine topics too. Nothing is excluded. I simply want students to focus on something that they are experts on.

There's more to choosing those topics, however. Without knowledge of their audience and purpose, students cannot position themselves as experts. In fact, depending upon the audience and purpose, students may not actually be experts. A student may consider herself an expert on soccer, but if the audience is soccer coaches, she may not be as confident about her knowledge. The assignment needs to provide more support and detail before students are able to choose their focus. I should help students identify a purpose and audience that will allow them to be authorities. I could assign both, but students will be more likely to maintain their position as experts (and will have more choice) if they identify their audience and goal for the project.

I still need to tackle the challenge of designing an assignment that pushes students beyond copying and rephrasing text from their resources. I have to shape the activity in such a way that students interact with the text and their subject knowledge rather than simply restate what they know. My solution for this class is to ask students to write FAQs (frequently asked questions) on topics that they choose themselves. The format will probably depart from the structure of the information that students will find in their research, and it will require them to reframe the information to meet the needs of a specific audience of readers.

Now that I've figured out the basic details for the assignment I want students to complete, I need to decide how to discuss the expectations for the assignment with the class and to make sure that I have all the supporting resources ready. Instead of passing out an assignment sheet to get things going, I'm going to ask students to identify their topics first by having them brainstorm lists of everything that they are experts in. In class I'll have them gradually narrow those lists and identify an audience of readers who would have questions about their areas of expertise. With that information determined, I'll share an assignment sheet that explains the project in more detail and points to additional resources. I'll create a rubric to guide assessment of the activity as well and then share this rubric with students when I pass out the assignment sheet. It's important that I make the connections between the assignment sheet and the grading criteria on the rubric clear from the beginning.

Models are very important to this assignment because I'm challenging students to compose a research paper in a genre that is probably new to them. I need to provide them with concrete examples of what the genre looks like. I'll search for example FAQs online, in books, and in brochures. Students will be encouraged to add examples to the class collection. I'll take time not only to look at the kind of information included in the models but also to talk about the grammatical structures and point of view in the questions and answers. We'll compare the models with the rubric for the activity to demonstrate the assessment criteria for the assignment.

Designing the supporting materials for this assignment means identifying models, creating a rubric, and pointing to grammatical details in the class handbook. When the due date approaches, we'll also complete a peer review activity, so I'll need to create a sheet of instructions to guide students' interaction. Some of this work I can do in advance, such as creating a cheat sheet that points to pertinent grammatical information in the class handbook. Other items, like the rubric, will grow from class exploration and discussion of examples and the assignment. I can sketch out the general categories for the assessment, but I'll wait until after we explore the genre in class before I make a final version.

The last thing that I'll probably do is finish the assignment sheet. I'll have a working draft early in the design process, but many of the final details depend upon other resources that I need to gather or create. I want to suggest the different kinds of writing and steps in the writing process that students should complete, and I'll use the assignment schedule to provide that scaffolding by indicating on it when the class will visit the library, when we'll look at the models, when students will share their drafts with each other in class, and when a draft is due for peer review. To tie things together, I'll probably include an FAQ section on the assignment sheet itself that deals with logistics like due dates and specific requirements, as well as provides resources such as details in the class handbook that students may want to consult as they write. I'll also point to the assessment rubric that I'll use to evaluate students' FAQs.

Once I have everything planned, I'll look back over the assignment resources to make sure that I have included everything necessary for a good assignment, using the "Three Goals for a Writing Assignment" to guide my analysis:

Defining the Task

- The FAQ format is asking for *critical thinking and interaction* with a text.

- Students are choosing topics and audiences that allow them to work as *experts* and that give them an *authentic* reason for communicating.

- The assignment asks students to *choose* the topic that they'll cover as well as the information that they will include about the topic in their FAQs.

Explaining the Expectations

- The assignment includes *models* and discussion of the *expectations* for the assignment.

- The *rubric* makes the criteria for the assessment clear.

Providing Support and Explanatory Materials

- The class will complete *peer review* and use a related *rubric* to focus on the requirements for the activity.

- The schedule included on the assignment sheet points out tasks for students to complete that will *scaffold the writing process* for them.

Designing an Expressive Assignment

Because I am teaching a writing course, I want students to spend time thinking about the decisions that they make as writers. The assignment I have in mind will focus primarily on expressive writing. I want students to explore their feelings as writers, reflect on their composing experiences, and share their thoughts on the way that they write.

A writer's log is a natural starting point. Many students read and write blog entries, using tools like Facebook, MySpace, and LiveJournal; all of them are curious about these writing spaces. I want to tap their interest in this kind of expressive writing, but I need an activity that will encourage them to identify and explore the challenges that they face as writers. I want them to move beyond restating what they've done as writers to thinking critically about their composing processes and strategies. I will compose a list of reflection questions that students can use to think about their writing. Students can respond to any of the questions, so there's plenty of choice for them. We can review the list and add questions as necessary later in the term.

This list of questions alone isn't a full writing assignment though. I need to provide more structure and support for the kind of writing I want students to do. Often a writer's log is read only by the writer and possibly by the teacher; however, I'd like students to interact with each other by reading one another's reflections. Publishing the logs online as blogs will make it easy for students to share their reflections, without the complication of making copies or attempting to pass around notebooks in class. The blog forms that students must fill out for their entries will also help ensure that all the basic requirements of the genre, like a title and the date, are included.

I check my district's acceptable use policy to see how the guidelines will affect the activity that I'm designing. The different software programs meet the basic requirements, and we can configure friend or buddy lists so that everyone in the class can read the entries, but people outside the class won't be able to access the information. In addition to providing a safer online experience, limiting the access also tightens the audience for the entries. Students will be writing only for themselves and for those of us in the class. Since we'll share background knowledge, students can focus on describing their individual composing experiences rather than on explaining the details of the other assignments they're discussing in these blogs.

As I begin creating an assignment sheet to explain this ongoing activity, I describe the basic goals and requirements of the entries and outline the logistics. In their comments, I want students to work together to analyze the techniques they try and to find new strategies. They can work as cheerleaders as well, encouraging one another throughout the semester. I'll add a section to the assignment sheet that describes this additional requirement for the writer's log: students won't just write entries but also read and respond to one another's entries. The commenting function in the blogging software will make this process easy, but I'll need to provide a lot of technical support in addition to explaining the writing requirements.

I have a good idea of the additional resources that I'm going to have to provide for the students now. They'll have the list of reflection questions, and they'll need access to computers and the Internet. I'll point to tutorials and documentation that explain basic HTML markup and the blogging site that we're using. These resources are comprehensive, but it may be hard for some students to find the information that they need. I'll design a blogging cheat sheet that will give students the basic details on how to use the site, and I'll also include a sheet that describes how to apply some of its special features, like adding an emoticon for the writer's mood or linking to the music that the writer was listening to while composing.

This assignment will be a bit different from a typical one because the end result won't be a polished paper. Feedback will be ongoing and informal, so I am going to limit the assessment materials to a checklist that outlines the basic requirements. I'll plan time in class to go over the checklist and talk about how it relates to the sample reflection questions. Students will naturally be experts at this activity—after all, they know more about the ways that they write than anyone else—but they will need a bit more information about what well-written blog entries look like. I'll share some model writer's log entries with the class and use those pieces to discuss the kinds of details and critical thinking that are expected for the entries and the related comments.

To expand the assessment for this activity, I'll also plan time to talk about blog comments and interaction as part of the assessment process. I want students to comment and interact as they follow one another's writing processes. It's likely that a number of students will be familiar with the process of commenting on a blog, but I can't assume that everyone knows how comments work. Even if students understand the technical process for adding a comment, they may not have considered what makes a comment effective. I'll create a list of sample comments for the class to discuss, and we'll work from that list to create some online discussion guidelines that will help them get started. I'll frame this discussion as formative assessment that involves the entire class in the evaluation process.

With these decisions made, I can review my plan to see if I've met the requirements of an effective writing assignment:

Defining the Task

- The list of questions encourages students to *think critically*, rather than simply reiterating the writing tasks that they have completed over the course of the week.

- Students will write for one another and use blog comments to respond to what they read, giving them a *clear audience of authentic readers*.

- Students will work as *experts*, since they know their own experiences well.

- The assignment includes a range of questions that students can *choose* among as they reflect on their writing experiences.

Explaining the Expectations

- A *checklist and models* will provide additional information on the requirements for the assignment.

- *Ongoing feedback* will be shared in the blog comments, which will increase students' understanding of the expectations and encourage them to improve their writing while also participating in the assessment of one another.

Providing Support and Explanatory Materials

- Cheat sheets and online resources will provide the *technical support resources* that students need for the activity.

- The format of the blog software provides some *scaffolding* for students by serving as a simple graphic organizer that ensures they include all the necessary parts for each entry.

Designing a Persuasive Assignment

I'm spending a few weeks on persuasive writing with this class, and it's time for students to shift to a more challenging persuasive message. We've written short persuasive paragraphs in class, but this will be their first full-length persuasive piece. I've noticed in these paragraphs that they need a strong sense of audience to write effectively in this genre, so I want to come up with an assignment that makes the relationship between the writer and the reader clear.

At the same time, I want the assignment to focus on standard persuasive strategies. These students need to strengthen their persuasive writing skills, which they'll be tested on later this term. I don't want the assignment to be too unusual, but I need to come up with something special to highlight the audience for the finished text. I would consider a number of options:

- Students could persuade readers to accept their point of view on a local issue in the news by writing letters to the editor or composing oral or video position statements for the local radio's public comment feature or for local public access television. Students could also publish their opinions online in podcasts or streaming video.

- Students could create brochures that persuade readers to take up a new hobby, visit a particular place, or adopt a specific point of view.

- Students could tackle editorials by writing columns for the school newspaper that persuade readers to change something about the school.

Any of these possible assignments would work, but I'm not sure that they provide the kind of message that would be right for this group of students.

Editorials and letters to the editor often have rather general audiences—everyone who reads the newspaper or listens to the radio station. That audience is so broad that I don't think it's the best starting place because this group of students needs a stronger, more specific group of readers. Persuasive brochures could work. Each student could focus the message on a specific group of people who fit the purpose of the brochure (e.g., someone who's never tried the hobby, who hasn't visited the place recently, or who either hasn't chosen a position or has the opposite point of view). I'm worried about choosing too many challenges in the assignment though. Students are not familiar with the nuances of brochure design, and I'd rather they focus on how audience affects persuasion than on learning a new format.

A persuasive letter is probably the best idea. The standard letter format will make the audience for the message clear, and the connections between the letter writer and the readers should be obvious to students. I just need to choose a kind of letter that has a stronger, more defined audience than a letter to the editor does. I'd do a little bit of research to gather possibilities: applications, requests and queries, recommendations, and endorsements.

Any of those options could work, but an endorsement letter may be best for this class. Students can work as experts by choosing a product or service that they use and then attempt to persuade readers to buy the same product or service for themselves. An endorsement letter would still follow a basic persuasive structure, but it would also provide the strong presence of the audience that this particular group of students needs. In addition, students have a lot of choice with this option, since they can select any product or service they want (within reason, of course). The activity should focus on critical thinking as well. Students won't be able simply to list product characteristics or features of a service: they'll have to do some critical thinking about the product or service to persuade their readers. Endorsement letters it is!

Now that I've identified the right task for this group of students, I'll have to determine the additional information they'll require to understand the expectations and complete the activity. They'll need lots of examples. Fortunately, we can include celebrity endorsements as we discuss the activity, and they'll be quite familiar with those. I'll add some sample endorsement letters as well. I'd like students to go through the examples and create a class list of the characteristics of the letters as well as the features that make some endorsements stand out as more convincing than others. To guide the assessment of the letters, we'll shape that class list into a checklist and rubric together, so I won't create those final documents in advance. I will go ahead and brainstorm a list for myself though, so that I can make sure that students catch all of the significant features as they review the letters.

As I compose the assignment sheet, I want to forecast the activities that we'll complete in class as we work on the assignment. We'll talk about the products and services a bit in the beginning to gather details that can be used in the endorsements. There will be a peer review day, when students will exchange letters and compare them to the characteristics on the class-generated rubric and checklist. I'll need to make a peer review sheet for that day. I'll include the page numbers to the section on letter writing in our class handbook as well, so that students know where to look up information on the format. We'll also use a persuasive writing graphic organizer so that students have a chance to think about the information in their letters in a context outside of the letter's format.

I think I've decided on all of the things that I need to provide for this lesson, so I will go through my notes one more time to make sure that I've included everything necessary for an effective writing assignment:

Defining the Task

- Writers will need to present the information in their letters so that readers are convinced to give the product or service a try. They won't be able simply to list details. They'll have to do *critical thinking* about the details, and they'll have to structure their letters so that those details are as persuasive as possible.

- The assignment has a *clear audience and purpose*—convincing people who might be interested in a product or service but who do not currently use it to try the product or service.

- Students will endorse products or services that they already use so that they communicate with their audience as *experts*.

- Students can *choose* any product or service to recommend, as long as it's appropriate for the classroom, and they can *choose* any level of formality that fits their audience and purpose.

Explaining the Expectations

- The class will explore a variety of *models* for endorsements from a range of different media (e.g., letters, radio/TV ads, websites).

- Students will compile lists of characteristics that we'll shape into a class *rubric* and *checklist*—that process will take care of *unpacking the meaning* of the assignment itself in addition to providing a statement of the expectations that will guide the assessment of students' letters.

Providing Support and Explanatory Materials

- The assignment sheet will include a schedule that suggests *steps in the writing process* that students can complete.

- The *peer review sheet* and discussion in class will provide additional structure for the writing process and focus extra attention on the importance of audience and purpose in this assignment.

- *Pointers to the class handbook and graphic organizers* will give students extra support as they work on their drafts in class and at home.

4 Defining New Tasks for Standard Writing Activities

The FAQs, writers' blogs, and endorsement letters in the previous chapter go beyond standard writing activities. They explore the same kinds of writing that more traditional assignments cover, but they focus on unusual or new alternatives for the standard kinds of writing that students are asked to complete. For many teachers, the challenge in designing writing assignments comes in identifying or inventing alternatives that depart from traditional assignments but still focus on traditional writing instruction and strategies.

In her chapter "Getting Ideas for Units and Making the Unit Blossom" in *Both Art and Craft: Teaching Ideas That Spark Learning*, Diana Mitchell outlines six different questions that she uses to frame assignments for her students:

- Can I change a point of view?
- Can I bring someone else in [to speak to the class]?
- Can I encourage students to think about characters in new ways?
- Can I encourage students to extend what is in the story?
- Can I identify new formats in which students can respond?
- Can I identify issues in stories that connect to the students' lives? (28–29)

Using these questions, Mitchell designs assignments that ask students to create missing narrative passages in novels, compose answering machine messages for characters in recent readings, and speculate on a fictional character's choice for a hero.

As I design writing assignments, I too try to define alternative writing tasks. Sometimes a twist on a traditional assignment comes to me quickly and easily, but often it takes a bit of thinking to arrive at an engaging and challenging new assignment that will still meet the goals for the class. To help with the invention process, I've created my own series of questions that encourages me to rethink and reframe traditional assignments. I rarely respond to all of the questions as I design an assignment, because changing every possible parameter could easily result in an awkward writing situation. Instead, I consider the various options, combining them as needed until I arrive at an assignment that fits the needs of the students I am teaching.

For each of my five questions, I'll explain how you can use the question to define a writing task for students. Each question is accompanied by example starting points that can be expanded into complete

- Who will read the text? Can I choose an alternative audience?
- What stance will students take as writers? Can the assignment ask for an unusual tone?
- When does the topic take place? Can the assignment focus on an alternative time frame?
- Where will the background information and detail come from? Can the assignment call for alternative research sources?
- Can students write something other than a traditional essay? Can the assignment call for alternative genres or publication media?

writing assignments. While I'm focusing on defining the writing task in this chapter, naturally I'll touch on the other goals for designing a writing assignment, which I discussed in Chapter 3, as they are appropriate. As you read through the examples, realize that a fully developed assignment would include more information than the simple prompts included here as starting points do.

Who will read the text? Can I choose an alternative audience?

In practice, it's possible that an assignment will be read only by those in the classroom, but the intended audience can be any one of a huge range of readers, as long as it is authentic and clearly explained for students. Figure 4.1 outlines many possible audiences for writing assignments—too many, in fact, for students to navigate on their own. The first task in using the list is to sort through the ideas to find the best options. You can choose specific readers in the various categories, or you can share several options and ask students to choose one audience or more for their work. Keep in mind that when you choose an authentic audience (assuming it's not a fictional audience for a literary project), you should help students send the final documents to the target audience as part of the activity. For example, if students write texts for local businesses, mail or hand-deliver the texts to those businesses.

When I search for alternative audiences for a writing activity, I try to narrow the choices for students and zero in on their expertise. If I begin with the audience "zoo visitors," for instance, I'd next think about whether that audience is identified specifically enough for students. Perhaps I should name a particular zoo or even individual animals in the zoo (e.g., everyone visiting the giant pandas at the National Zoo). I

Alternative Audiences for Writing Assignments

School-Related
- students in other classes
- teachers
- department chair or members
- librarians
- advisors/guidance counselors
- administrators
- support staff
- family members of students
- school graduates
- athletic team members, coaches, and sponsors
- school clubs and organizations
- club and organization sponsors
- students at other local schools (at the same or another academic level)
- students at schools in geographically different locations or that serve a different population of students
- accreditation organizations
- funding organizations (e.g., those providing grants funds)

K–12 Schools
- local school board
- district administrators
- state or federal department of education

Colleges/Universities
- deans
- department chair
- provost or president
- board of visitors or board of trustees

Employment-Related
- co-workers
- managers
- business owners
- franchise or corporation administrators
- customers
- vendors or suppliers

Recreation-Related
- zoo and museum staff, visitors, volunteers, donors, and supporters
- staff and volunteers at state and national parks and historical sites
- recreation program managers, organiz-ers, participants, and supporters (e.g., Little League, YWCA)

Local
- community organizations—clubs, churches, and so forth
- businesses and corporations
- recreational groups and sports clubs or teams
- library staff
- city officials (including elected officials)
- election candidates and politicians
- senior center residents or visitors
- chapters of nonprofit organizations (e.g., American Heart Association or Girl Scouts of the United States of America)
- food bank donors, employees, volunteers, and managers
- convention and visitors' bureau
- chamber of commerce
- chapter of the Better Business Bureau

State and National
- government officials (including elected officials)
- election candidates and politicians
- corporations and other businesses—employees, managers, officers, stock holders, boards of directors
- nonprofit and philanthropic organizations

Personal
- students themselves—in the past or future
- family members (including extended family members)
- family friends
- friends

Literary-Related
- characters in the text or in another reading
- the author of the text
- historical figures from the time period
- others who have read the text
- critics who have reviewed the text

Designing Writing Assignments by Traci Gardner ©2008 National Council of Teachers of English.

Figure 4.1. Teachers should help students navigate this list of audiences.

also need to think about students' experiences—have they all visited a zoo? If students don't have the expertise to write for the specific audience, I need to choose something different or widen the audience. Switching from the audience of "zoo visitors" to "people who visit the zoo or the zoo website" expands the options so that every student should have adequate expertise, especially if I add time in the schedule for the class to explore the zoo's website.

Choice is important in defining the writing task. When possible, I look for more than one group of readers so that I can give students several options to choose among. For instance, I might offer students the option of writing to a city official, a local political candidate, a law enforcement officer, or a community organization president. Students would then choose one of these general audiences and finally narrow the audience even further to the specific person or people who will actually read the text (e.g., Blacksburg, Virginia, Chief of Police Kimberley S. Crannis).

The following starting points show how one topic—explaining a new rule or program at the school—can be positioned for a range of alternative audiences. Regardless of the audiences I choose, I need to be sure to position students as experts, so I would structure time in the schedule for students to talk about the rule or program in class. We would explore the details as much as necessary to ensure that every student understands the rule or program well enough to explain it clearly and can discuss how it affects students, school staff, family members, and visitors to the school. For each starting point below, I add details on the ways that the choice of audience influences other aspects of the complete writing assignment.

- *Explain a new rule or program to the families of students who attend your school and try to convince them to support it.* As I develop an assignment from this starting point, I'd spend time in class asking students to think about the questions that families will have and how the rule or program will affect them. To move students beyond simple restatement in their writing, I'd encourage them to reframe the information so that it fits this family perspective, rather than the student-oriented point of view included in the original statement of the rule or program. As a class, we'd gather a list of characteristics important to the message, and, for models, we'd look at other messages sent home to families. To make the activity more authentic, I'd ask students to share their messages with their own families. Alternately, we might compare the different versions written by students and create one class version to send home.

- *Write to local businesses to explain a new program or rule at your school and ask them to support it.* To prepare students to write for this audience, we'd spend time in class brainstorming local businesses and ways that they might support the new program or rule. The activity gives students a number of options because of the support different businesses will be able to offer. To reframe the activity so that it moves beyond restating the description of the rule or program, I'd ask students to consider how the businesses will be affected by the rule and ask them to compose an explanation that fits with the businesses' points of view. After the messages have been written and students have received feedback from peer reading groups, students will deliver the messages to the businesses.

- *Imagine that a character from a piece of literature you have read is transported to your school. Describe the new program or rule to the character so that he or she understands and can follow it.* This starting point requires some creative thought from students, so I'd add time for brainstorming, freewriting, and small-group discussion of the fictional characters and the ways those characters would react to the new program or rule. Depending upon the character, students may need to completely rethink the new rule or program as they explain it—imagine, for instance, how one of Chaucer's pilgrims would react to a rule regarding the use of MP3 players at the school. I'd schedule time to talk about language and historical considerations and ensure that students have the supporting information and resources that they need. I'd add a reflective component to the assignment that asks students to explain how they chose their characters and why they explained the program or rule in the ways that they did. I'd also have students share their pieces with others in the class who have read the same texts.

What stance will students take as writers? Can the assignment ask for an unusual tone?

Students need to be positioned as experts in their writing, but you can customize the tone they use as they share their expertise. Begin with one of the possible positions outlined in Figure 4.2. As I design an assignment with an alternative tone, I scan through the list and choose positions that ask students to move beyond basic informal or formal tones. Depending upon the activity, I'd either choose specific positions for students to take or decide to share the entire list with the class. Either way, I'd spend time unpacking the different stances on the list with the class. While the differences among the positions are probably clear to me, they may not be evident to students.

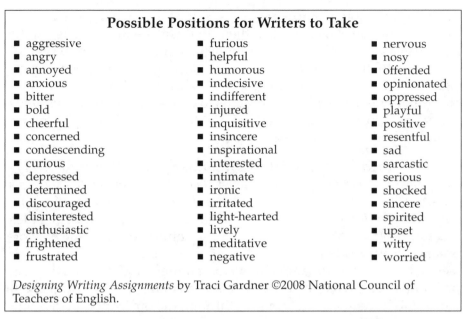

Figure 4.2. These positions will push students to be more adventurous.

In addition to making sure that students can define the relevant stances, I'd spend time asking them to compare the positions and to think about how the stance would affect the messages they are to complete. Take, for instance, the words *angry, annoyed, furious, irritated,* and *upset.* With such a group of related words, I'd ask students to arrange them on a continuum and play out the ways that each position would change someone's reaction in an example situation (e.g., learning that a store will not refund money for a computer game). I'd have students work through an example scenario or two in small groups, perhaps presenting skits that demonstrate the situation for the full class. After working through the samples as a class, students will have a concrete model of the kind of thinking they need to do as they compose.

Freewriting and other informal writing are also important when students write from alternative positions, so I'd include time for students to gather ideas on those perspectives in their journals before they begin their drafts. Writing from a specific position gives students the chance to try on the voice for their messages. Just as important as having students try on the position that they will use for their work is having them write informally from an opposing position. For instance, after freewriting from the position of someone confident about applying for a job, I'd ask students to write in the voice of someone nervous about applying for a job. Comparing notes from the two stances gives students details that can strengthen their final drafts—the language of the nervous writer shouldn't appear in the text of the confident writer!

The following scenarios provide starting points for writing assignments that ask for different tones. When possible, it's best to include more than one tone for students to choose from, so that students can adopt a position that feels comfortable. For each starting point, I'd include details on the full assignment that I'd develop.

- *The local city council has announced a new ordinance concerning bicycle helmets. Write a persuasive letter that asks the council to change its decision. Choose a tone—concerned, frustrated, anxious, or serious—that communicates your feelings about the new rule.* To move from this starting idea to a full assignment, I'd begin with lots of information on the new ordinance itself. Students cannot do a good job of communicating their feelings about the ordinance if they don't understand it, so we'd spend time unpacking what the ordinance means both literally and personally to the students. After working through the ordinance, I'd ask students to either freewrite or brainstorm about ways that the ordinance could affect them. This process will provide students with concrete details to support their tone. With all this supporting background information in hand, students will begin composing their messages. As appropriate, in minilessons I'd talk about how they can include supporting details in their messages. When the messages are finished, I'd gather them all and deliver them to the city administration building.

- *Write a letter from one character in a reading to another from that same reading that communicates the person's feelings about a significant plot event. Use the tone that is appropriate for the character's perspective.* Before students can begin communicating a character's feelings they need to choose the plot event to focus on. To get started, I'd have students get into their literature circles to brainstorm significant events from the reading. Once each group has a list of events, I'd have group members review the lists and decide if they are all significant events. I'd encourage discussion of what makes an event significant to the plot. Because this list of events will be crucial to the writing process, I'd make sure that every group member copies the list. Once students have a list of events to choose from, I'd ask them to freewrite some journal entries from the perspective of the character they choose for their letter. To structure the entries a bit, I'd ask students to write an entry that shows the character's feelings before the plot event, during the plot event, and after the plot event. Students can share these journals with their literature circles, and as a class we'd use these first notes to begin a class rubric that accounts for how the letters will communicate the character's feelings. I'd also spend time talking about audience and purpose for the messages, so that students think about how they can communicate the character's feelings to another character in an appropriate way. Once the letters are finished, I'd provide summative comments, guided by the rubric the class has developed.

When does the topic take place? Can the assignment focus on an alternative time frame?

Some assignments can be customized simply by adding or changing the relevant time. Instead of merely asking students to describe a place that is significant to them, frame the time period to sharpen their focus: describe a significant childhood place or describe a place that has been important to you during this school year. Figure 4.3 suggests some alternative time frames that can inspire creative assignments.

For each of the time periods, I'd have students research or gather the background information that will position them as experts. In some cases, students can simply gather their own memories in journal entries. Other times, however, they may need to talk to family, community members, or friends who were present during the time. Library research might be important if students are writing about an era that doesn't have personal relevance. If students are writing about the time period in a text they have read (such as when a novel is set), students can collect details about that period. For all this research, I'd try to provide graphic organizers and other scaffolding to help students gather everything that they will need to produce an effective piece of writing.

The format that students use may deserve special attention when they write about different time periods as well—after all, it wouldn't make sense for a student to compose a series of email messages when writing from the perspective of Renaissance England (unless, of course, such an anachronistic situation is part of the assignment). I would talk with students about the different genres that would be appropriate for the relevant time period and provide additional support for any genres that are unfamiliar. This exploration of genres can fold neatly into the background research that students complete for the assignment, so that it becomes a natural discussion for the class.

For each of the example starting points below, I suggest how I would provide ways for students to gather background information as I worked from the issues raised during class discussions to develop the full assignment:

Alternative Time Frames for Assignments

General
- a number of years in the past or the future
- an hour earlier or later
- a day earlier or later
- a week earlier or later
- over the course of a day, week, month, or year
- during a decade

Personal
- childhood—a particular age or generally
- a particular year of school
- time spent at a particular school
- days, weeks, months, or years in the future or past
- before, during, or after a holiday or significant event

Historical
- before, during, or after a significant event
- before, during, or after a figure's life or a significant event in that figure's life

Literary
- just before or after a plot event
- just before the events in the text begin
- just after the events in the text end
- a different literary time period
- a character's life five years earlier or later
- the first person to ever read the text
- the last person to ever read the text

Designing Writing Assignments by Traci Gardner ©2008 National Council of Teachers of English.

Figure 4.3. Selecting an atypical time frame will inspire creativity.

- *What was important about the time you spent in kindergarten? Describe a significant event and demonstrate why the event mattered to you.* Students will probably remember specific details about their early education, so I would begin with some prewriting questions that tap those memories. When I introduce the activity to students, I'd be careful to talk about alternative time periods so that students who did not attend kindergarten still feel confident about working on the assignment. If the students in the class had extremely varied backgrounds, I might even adjust the assignment to focus on "the first day/week/month of school." After students gather their memories from their early school days, I'd ask them to identify two or three events to focus on and brainstorm reasons that the events were significant to them. If possible, I'd have students talk to family members about the event also, with the idea of determining if others remembered the events the same way that they do.

■ *If you could look in your crystal ball and determine the most signifi-cant thing that happened to you this week, what would it be? Write a cause-and-effect paper that explains what the event is and predicts how it will affect you.* It's easy for students to remember things that happen during the current week, but it's harder to determine why or if those events are significant. For this task, I'd begin designing the assignment by unpack-ing the writing prompt. Although students probably know what the word *significance* means literally, it's useful to talk about what makes an event significant and how we decide whether something is signifi-cant to us. After that discussion, I would model the process of brain-storming a list of events and evaluating the list items to find the most significant events. Choosing a specific event from another point in time works well, so I might make a list of events from summer vacation and then narrow the list down to significant ones. I'd also spend time de-fining and exploring what a cause-and-effect paper is and conjecture the possible effects of the events that the students choose. I'd encour-age students to choose a specific time in the future because a concrete future time, such as the first day of a new job, will help students iden-tify the particular effects of the events. During a minilesson, I'd spend time covering transitions that students can use in their writing. Early in the process, I'd share a rubric that touched on both defining signifi-cant events and exploring the effects of an event, and I'd return to the rubric periodically as students work on their papers, so that the con-nections between their writing and its assessment are clear.

■ *If the novel that you have read were set during the American Civil War, how would the protagonist's life be different? Write a paper that explains the general differences to the protagonist and provides concrete examples of ways that specific plot events would change.* This assignment actually begins when students choose the books for independent reading. My goal is to connect to the content area information students have been study-ing in their history class to their reading content, but I want them to complete an activity that moves beyond simply stating facts from a his-torical fiction text set during the Civil War. I'd begin by providing a list of novels with contemporary settings, and then I'd discuss the require-ment for such a setting and pass out an assignment sheet or explain the writing task before students choose their books, so that they understand the purpose of the setting requirement. Because the book choice is so important, I'd ask students to turn in a brief note with the author and title of the book as well as a few sentences that tell me the time period the book covers. By reviewing these notes, I can intervene if a student chooses a book that will not work well for the assignment. I'd provide a graphic organizer to encourage students to take notes on details in the novel that might be different if the novel were set during the American Civil War. Because knowledge of the Civil War is vital to this activity, I'd have the class work in small groups to create cheat sheets on the time period, using their notes and texts from the history class. Each group would focus on a different topic (e.g., the role of women, life for African Americans, military battles) and then share the finished cheat sheets with the rest of the class.

Where will background information and detail come from?

Regardless of whether students are writing research papers, you can tweak the sources that they use and thereby create alternatives to traditional writing assignments. The list of alternative resources in Figure 4.4 demonstrates the overwhelming range of options. To create your own twists on generic assignments, just go through the list of alternatives and think about how they might be used as a resource for details. When I choose prospective sources, I always begin with availability. If students do not have easy access to the different texts, they will struggle with the writing activity. If the resources are readily available in the school library, I can move forward without worry. In other cases, I may provide examples myself. For instance, if students need access to children's picture books, I can check out copies from the public library and make them available in the classroom and on reserve in the school library. If there is ever a question about access, I will include an option for more than one resource so that students can choose a text that they can easily acquire.

My concern is not solely physical accessibility when I look for options for students' work. Students must have the literacy skills necessary to read and critique the texts. If the text calls for more sophisticated strategies than students are likely to develop quickly or already have, the text is not a good choice. If students have had no experiences with almanacs, for instance, they aren't a good option for this kind of alternative assignment.

Once the question of which sources to use has been addressed, I'd move on to exploring the texts themselves. Students may be familiar with many of these research sources, but they often have not taken the time to think critically about the characteristics of the texts. Using a sample text, I would walk students through the text structures, asking questions that compare the text to other sources students are familiar with. I might compare a coffee-table book to a history textbook or

Alternative Research Sources for Assignments

- almanacs
- anthologies
- artworks
- atlases
- audio recordings
- bibliographies
- biographies and autobiographies
- blogs
- board games
- book or movie reviews
- buildings
- catalogs
- census data
- children's picture books
- chronologies, chronicles, and timelines
- coffee-table books
- computer operating systems
- concerts
- concordances
- databases
- dictionaries
- discussion forums
- drawings and illustrations
- email messages
- experiments
- eyewitness accounts
- folk stories
- grave markers
- historical documents
- hypertexts
- instant messages/chat rooms
- Internet archives
- interviews
- introductions or guides
- journal articles
- letters
- library catalogs
- lyrics
- magazine articles
- memos
- monuments
- movies
- musical scores
- newsgroups
- newspapers
- nonfiction books
- novels
- obituaries
- observations
- online encyclopedias
- oral presentations
- pamphlets and brochures
- performances (music, dance, etc.)
- personal communications
- personal journals, logs, or diaries
- personal memories
- photographs
- plays
- poems
- postcards
- PowerPoint or KeyNote presentations
- public records
- quotations
- reenactments
- religious texts
- reports
- search engines
- software documentation
- software programs
- statistics
- statues
- surveys
- telephone books
- television programs
- textbooks
- thesauruses
- travel guidebooks
- video games
- websites
- wikis
- yearbooks
- zines

Designing Writing Assignments by Traci Gardner ©2008 National Council of Teachers of English.

Figure 4.4. Teachers should determine which alternative research sources can be accessed by students and which ones will require additional text-reading skills.

compare almanacs and encyclopedias to Wikipedia. After looking at larger features, I'd ask students to focus on issues like the use of language, the formatting of the text, and how illustrations are used.

Finally, as I define the writing task for students, I'd ask them to use the resources in ways that go beyond restating information from the text. I'd ask students to use the text to generate questions about something else that they are reading. Students might use newspapers from the 1930s to gather questions about *The Grapes of Wrath*, or they could use soldiers' eyewitness accounts from World War I to shape their inquiry of *All Quiet on the Western Front.* Sometimes I ask students to use research sources to explain something mentioned elsewhere. I've asked students to choose an allusion from a poem they are reading and use a religious text or collection of folk stories to explain why the author used the allusion. Other times, the unusual research sources offer inspiration for students' own writing. A historical monument, roadside marker, or grave marker might inspire a creative narrative about the related person or event.

The sample starting points below demonstrate how I would move from the starting idea to define a writing task and develop a full writing assignment.

- *Ask students to tell the story behind a coffee-table book.* From this beginning idea, I'd think about all the ways students might tell a story. They could tell an imagined tale of how the coffee-table book came into being, a narrative of how and why an imagined character acquired the book, or even a creative tale of what the coffee table thinks of the book. I'd either leave the options wide open or narrow the task further to fit the needs of a particular group of students. Once the general task is defined, I'd bring in some examples of coffee-table books and talk about the genre with the class. Together, we'd create a class definition of the genre and sketch out a list of common characteristics. If students are comfortable with the genre, we'd spend a day in the school library for students to self-select books from the collection. If students need a bit more support, I'd choose books with the librarian and set aside a pile of appropriate ones for students to choose from. If students choose books independently, I'd ask them to show their choices to me before they get too involved in the project, just to ensure that they all have chosen texts that fit the genre. With texts selected and the genre explored, students are ready to begin writing and revising.

- *Have students gather opinions on current events by searching blogs and forum postings and then write a paper that presents at least two different views of the issue and how the writer's perspective influences the facts included in the postings.* Before fleshing out a writing task that taps online resources, I'd confirm that the activity fits with the school's acceptable use policy and create a list of online resources for students to use. If school policy allows, students can use search engines to find blogs and forum postings on their own, but I'd still have a backup list of appropriate blogs and forums. Since the activity focuses on current events, I'd begin by asking students to brainstorm some local, state, national, and international events from the news. I'd ask students to narrow the lists by eliminating items that are unlikely to evoke differing opinions. At the same time, I'd have students talk about the various opinions and positions that people discussing the remaining topics might express. Using sample blog entries, I'd explore the differences between subjective and objective information in the posts, and we'd also discuss the importance of evaluating the reliability of sources. With this information in place, I'd have students begin choosing resources for their papers. Once students have gathered some blog or forum posts, I'd demonstrate how to identify facts in some sample posts and then compare the facts from different texts. Depending upon the topics that students are pursuing, I might bring in resources to supplement their work. For instance, if a student is examining a current debate on free speech, I'd point the student to the Bill of Rights online as well as to ACLU resources on First Amendment rights. With the process modeled and their resources collected, students can begin the process of writing a comparison of the different sources. I'd discuss comparison and contrast writing strategies in minilessons as they work on their drafts and then I'd share details on the expectations for the activity.

Can students write something other than a traditional essay? Can the assignment call for alternative genres or publication media?

You can renovate an assignment completely by rethinking the final texts students create. The most basic assignment is the traditional essay printed out, by hand or computer, on sheets of paper. Change the genre, the publication medium, or both to create an unusual assignment. Figure 4.5 outlines dozens of genres and subgenres that can enliven a writing activity. The different genres and subgenres are not equal in their writing challenges or requirements. When I choose alternative publication genres, I begin with those that students are likely to be familiar with. If I choose a genre that students have little or no experience with, they probably will not do their best writing. I also have to think about the other writing activities that students will complete in the course,

Alternative Genres and Subgenres for Assignments

- acrostic
- advertising giveaway—buttons, pens, calendars, etc.
- almanac article
- anagram
- anthology or submission to a class anthology
- application (e.g., job, college, grant)
- bad news letter or memo
- banner ad
- billboard
- blank verse
- blog—personal, corporate, etc.
- book cover or dust jacket
- bulletin board (on the wall)
- business card
- campaign speech
- cartoon
- CD or DVD collection (e.g., the items in the collection)
- CD or DVD cover
- census report
- chart, diagram, or graph
- cinquain
- claims letter
- classified ad (e.g., personal, want ad)
- coffee-table book
- collage—word, visual, aural
- collections letter
- comic book or strip
- commercial (radio, television, or online)
- congratulatory letter
- contract
- cookbook or recipe collection
- cover story or front page news
- crossword puzzle
- declaration
- dialogue
- diamante
- diary entry
- dictionary or dictionary entry
- direct mail—letter, pamphlet, post-card, etc.
- directory (e.g., staff, telephone, member)
- dramatic monologue
- dramatic scene or skit

- eBay listing
- editorial column
- email message—personal, customer service, interoffice, etc.
- eulogy
- expository essay
- eyewitness account
- fake news—comedic or corporate/government-produced
- feature article
- flyer, pamphlet, or brochure
- found poem
- free verse
- friendly/personal letter
- fund-raising letter
- game instructions
- good news letter or memo
- government report
- grave marker/tombstone
- greeting card—birthday, holiday, condolence, thank you, etc.
- grocery list
- haiku
- homepage on a website
- hospital chart
- illustration
- IM or chat room transcript
- infomercial
- interview or interview transcript
- item description for a mail-order catalog
- item description for an online store
- letter of recommendation
- letter or memo of introduction
- letter poem
- limerick
- list, or catalogue, poem
- log entry
- lyrics and/or music—pop, country, western, ballad, heavy metal, rap, etc.
- magazine or journal ad
- map with legend
- math problem
- meeting transcript
- memo—departmental or interoffice
- memoir
- memo of understanding
- menu

continued on next page

Figure 4.5. Assignments can focus on genres of differing complexity and length.

Figure 4.5 continued

- monologue
- monument or statue
- MP3 player playlist
- newsgroup posting or thread
- newspaper ad (e.g., full to partial page ad for businesses, etc.)
- newspaper or magazine insert
- news teaser
- notebook
- obituary
- ode
- online bulletin board posting or thread
- online forum posting
- online profile (such as on Facebook or MySpace)
- PA announcement
- pantoum
- performance appraisal
- personal commentary
- personal interest article (as in newspapers, magazines, etc.)
- photo gallery/album
- photograph with caption, key- words/tags, and/or descriptions
- picture book
- play
- police report—CSI-style, coroner's, moving violation ticket, etc.
- political advertisement
- pop-up ad
- postcard
- poster
- press release
- product or service website
- product placement recommendation (e.g., placement in movie or TV show)
- proposal
- public service announcement
- quiz
- ransom note
- recipe
- recipe poem
- recommendation report
- reference book or entry/article in a reference book
- report card
- resignation letter or memo
- resume
- sales letter
- sandwich board
- scrapbook
- script—television, radio, podcast, etc.
- short story
- social worker's report
- sonnet
- special news report or update
- sports score and story
- survival kit
- tanka
- telegram
- telemarketer's script
- telephone book ad
- testimonial ad/endorsement
- text message
- thank you letter, memo, or note
- timeline
- trading card
- transcript of phone call, conversa- tion, etc.
- transit ad (i.e., ad on bus, plane, or train)
- treaty
- trip report
- T-shirt message
- video or computer game vignette
- villanelle
- voice mail message
- wanted poster
- warning sign
- Web page—personal, corporate, organization, educational, etc.
- wiki or wiki entry
- will
- word seek puzzle
- yearbook—spread on student life, class section, feature on academics, special profile, sports section, ad, or special event
- zine

since writing instruction must cover a wide range of genres and texts of differing complexity and length. I try to build activities from least to most sophisticated, so a more complicated genre like a telemarketer's script or a villanelle would be more appropriate later in the term.

The range of genres included in Figure 4.5 includes many that are fairly traditional, with their emphasis on words, sentences, and paragraphs. Writing letters or memos, dialogues, short poems, and newspaper articles are good places to start because they are most likely to match students' prior experiences as writers. More sophisticated tasks ask for genres that are less familiar to students—such as campaign speeches, declarations, or police reports. Perhaps the most sophisticated genre options ask for multimodal composition, which can involve still pictures, words, sounds, and moving images. Even an assignment as simple as designing a bumper sticker asks students to think about the use of color, layout, and the interplay of words and images. As I make choices of genres for students, I try to match the activity to the students and to build on the abilities that students have already demonstrated. Additionally, I add a genre study as part of the exploration of the expectations for the assignment to help ensure that students understand the task before them.

I also talk about the medium for students' composition. In some cases, the genre determines the medium. For instance, a banner ad or pop-up ad is designed for online presentation on a Web page. You just won't find pop-up ads in your print newspaper. Other genres lend themselves to several media—a testimonial ad could be an audio recording, a video recording, or a print design. As you scan through the list of genres and subgenres, consider how students might publish their work as an audio recording, a Web page, an animation, a video recording, a hypertext, a computer-based presentation (including a PowerPoint or KeyNote presentation), or a series of still visual images.

In many cases, the critical thinking that students do for more sophisticated genres may not be obvious in the final version of their work. Are all the decisions that go into designing a bumper sticker going to be evident simply by looking at the final product? Probably not. To ensure that the thinking behind students' work is clear, I typically add an artist's journal in which students explain the options that they considered and the reasons for their final decisions.

The following possible starting points demonstrate how I would think through the design and support for writing assignments that ask students to work in unusual genres.

▪ *Imagine one of your most important belongings has been stolen. Create a police report that describes the item with enough detail for officers to identify the object if they recover it.* This writing task is basically a description of a tangible object. I hope to have students focus their attention on crucial details by working in the format of a police report. The genre actually determines the audience—the police officers who will look for the object—and purpose—to provide enough information to help the police find and identify the object—for their writing as well. I'd try to have the school's resource officer or a city police officer visit the class to talk about the process of reporting a stolen object, or I'd at least try to get a sample copy of the forms that the local police department uses. With this information, the class and I can craft both graphic organizers and a rubric or checklist for the activity. I'd spend some time talking about the objects that students choose for this assignment. I want to be sure that students choose an item that's appropriate for class discussion as well as one that is not overly personal. I'd suggest a number of options and then ask students to brainstorm additional items as a class or in small groups. In case students are uncomfortable talking about an item of their own, I'd also include some options for items in the school that might work for the activity, such as a library book or one of my own belongings in the classroom.

▪ *Design an eBay listing for a significant object that the main character in a recent text you have read has decided to sell. Remember to include images, descriptions, shipping information, and pricing.* To develop a full writing assignment from this starting point, I'd begin with the books that students are reading. This activity can work as a book report alternative for individuals or as a group project for books read in literature circles. I'd wait until students have read a third to half of the book before introducing the activity. At that point, I'd explain the activity and have students brainstorm lists of three to four significant objects from the book that the character might be willing to sell. With potential objects identified, I'd provide a bookmark graphic organizer that students would use to track details on the object from the book. First, students would track back through the book, looking for pertinent details and noting them on their bookmarks. As they continue reading, they add the information that they find. Once students finish reading their books, I'd share several examples of eBay listings that show a range of effectiveness. I'd ask students to work in small groups to compare the eBay examples and determine characteristics of effective listings. After sharing the characteristics with the class, we'd work together to shape a checklist and rubric that would be used to describe the objects. I'd add minilessons on specific aspects that fit the criteria. For instance, I'd likely talk about the differences between objective and subjective descriptions and about how the two different kinds of description are used in the listings.

    ■ *Create a visual collage of belonging that is important to you, your family, or your community. Your collage should communicate your feelings about the belonging.* Because students may be less familiar with composing multimodal texts, I'd begin this activity with discussion of several example collages, asking questions about the feelings students associate with the images and having students conjecture on the artist's purpose for including the different images in the collage. Only after students have seen several models would I introduce the actual assignment. To help ensure that students think through the decisions for their collages, I'd add some specific structures to support their process. We'd first talk about appropriate objects for the activity and brainstorm twenty to thirty possibilities. I'd emphasize, of course, that students can choose items that are not on the list. I'd have students choose an item to focus on and then spend some time freewriting about why they chose the item as well as their feelings about that object. This freewriting will be the first entry in an artist's journal that each student will keep. After each class period and after working on the collage out of class, I'd ask students to note what they chose to include or change and to explain the decisions that they have made. To focus students' collages on communicating their feelings about their belongings, I'd limit the images of the actual object that each collage includes, because one to three photos or illustrations should be enough. I'd allow plenty of class time for students to search for additional text and images to include in their collages. I'd provide computer access so that students can look for items online, and I'd have old magazines and newspapers in the classroom for students to work from. When the collages are complete, I'd ask students to review their artist's journals and compose short artist's statements to accompany their collages. I'd allow class time for a showing of the collages with the posted artist's statements. If possible, I'd display the collages on a school bulletin board or in the classroom.

5 Preparing for Standardized Testing

The prompts that students face on standardized tests are the antithesis of effective writing assignments. They rarely include any true choice for students, who are clearly not engaged as equals in the writing task. There is little in the way of scaffolding, and the usual writing process that students use is essentially ignored. Correct form may be preferred over any attempt at critical thinking. Indeed, students may not have the time to engage in any kind of deep thought as they hurriedly rush to beat the clock. Any sense of audience is left for students to discover (or, more accurately, completely invent). There's no feedback and no discussion of the grading criteria. At the end of the test period, the work disappears to be replaced weeks later with a number that gives students no sense of how the piece was evaluated or what they did well. In short, the writing prompts on standardized tests poorly define the task, do not explain that task or the related expectations, and do not provide any support for students.

Standardized writing prompts clearly do not match the characteristics of effective writing assignments. Given that well-developed writing assignments result in good writing, it's not surprising that the less-developed prompts typically used in standardized writing assignments result in weaker writing. Further, the curricular focus on test preparation can result in ineffective writing instruction throughout the year. Gregory Shafer describes the effects of standardized essay tests on the students who take them: "In this high-stakes and decidedly daunting environment, students abandon certain ideas about writing and embrace more reductive and less active approaches. If schools value linear, product-based steps, then students are going to see writing as an act that is quick, devoid of stages, impersonal, and predicated upon the values of a single authority. They are going to cease to see it as a social activity that is read by an authentic audience, and they are going to stop seeing writing as an act of artistic creation" (241). It's not hard to understand why students draw these conclusions. If the only writing that counts is composed in a frantic twenty-five to thirty minutes, why would students value freewriting, structural revision, or rough drafts that take days to develop?

It's a frustrating situation. Everything that goes into designing effective writing assignments seems unrelated to the assignments students encounter on standardized writing tests. I know that I cannot magically turn a standardized test prompt into an effective assignment, but I *can* apply the three aspects of effective design to one by working through activities that help students learn to define the task, explore the expectations for that task, and provide supportive materials for completing the task.

Defining the Task

I don't know the exact question students will see on a standardized test in advance, but I do know a great deal about the different ways that people write. Further, the general task for test essays is already defined—students will write a timed essay in response to an unknown prompt. They will not have any prewriting notes to draw on. They can usually make some quick notes in the test booklet, but because of the time crunch, they need to work on a complete draft of their response as soon as possible.

Depending upon the test, there are sample responses, rubrics, and sample prompts that I can use to prepare the class. Even more important, by the time students come to my classroom for this preparation, they have already had many experiences with in-class or timed writing, such as papers written during a class period, essays for other standardized tests, or short-answer questions on tests. I can tap this prior experience as I shape a standardized test prompt into a more effective writing assignment by asking students to identify what they do when they compose responses during timed writing situations and then challenge them to determine which strategies work best for them in which situations.

Scaffolding the Process

To write effectively on standardized tests, students need to be conscious of how they write under pressure. I ask students to recall their previous in-class writing experiences by brainstorming a list of times they have had to write quickly in class (e.g., on unit tests or semester exams). Once they have a list to draw on, I ask students to think about what they recall from these timed writing experiences, encouraging them to explore both the concrete facts about their writing and the feelings they had while they were writing. As students share their memories, I try to draw particular attention to similarities and differences among their memories as well as the reasons that the memories have stayed with them.

To tie test writing situations to other composing that they have done, I next have students brainstorm a list of all the things they write. If they have difficulty getting started on their personal lists, I offer some suggestions—journal writing, tests, email messages, letters, blog entries, shopping lists, and so forth (refer to Figure 4.5 for more genres). Once students have compiled personal lists, they work in small groups to examine what they've identified. As they compare their lists, I ask them to think about what these different kinds of writing have in common with one another and with test writing. When we turn to full class discussion, I highlight the similarities that tie directly to writing and the writing process.

Focusing on the writing process in this way is key. Standardized writing tests draw on different processes than those that students typically use for composing, but these tests still involve a writing process. Once students recognize the range of options available, it's simpler to ask them to identify the writing strategies they can use in test situations.

I next ask students to choose three different kinds of writing from the lists that they have created and write a paragraph or so in their journals that narrates how they compose in each circumstance as well as a paragraph on writing essays on standardized tests. When they finish writing about each of these processes, I arrange students in groups again and ask them to compare the different processes that they all follow. I ask students to draw conclusions about the different processes and how they relate to the different genres, audiences, and situations explored in their writing. Throughout their discussion, I try to encourage students to recognize that while the different aspects of the writing process change, writers always have a process to compose their texts.

Exploring the Task and Expectations

I also need to focus directly on the task and the expectations for students' work—beginning by unpacking the meaning behind the prompts on standardized tests. Learning to read the writing prompts on these tests is essential to success. Standardized writing tests generally use the language of academic discourse and in some cases begin with literary quotations. I spend time in class analyzing example test prompts by focusing on the following activities:

- asking students to identify the audience and purpose behind the prompts (going beyond the simplistic answer of the testing company, of course)
- having students identify what readers will look for and how they can present themselves as experts on the issue
- demonstrating how to search through each writing prompt for significant words—both those that give clues to the content expected in response and those that suggest the structure and genre required
- showing students how to find clues to the content and scope required by each prompt as well as to the organization and development that will be necessary for the response

As part of this analysis, I pass out copies of the Prompt Analysis Chart in Figure 5.1, which students complete to explore the task in a structured way. As is appropriate for the different kinds of test prompts, I talk in more detail about how the audience can be defined for the activity. If an audience is mentioned or implied, it's important to show students how to locate the information in the prompt, just as they would with any other writing assignment. In instances where there is no mention of the readers, we spend time defining the audience by examining the content and purpose of the test and the writing task. Additionally, I always discuss how using personal knowledge about the topic will strengthen their work by positioning them as experts.

With the prompt discussed, I turn to the expectations for the test by exploring available rubrics and sample essays. The class reads through the model answers, applying the rubrics that we have available. As they analyze these texts, I ask students both to identify the successful features of the models and to suggest ways to improve the sample responses.

Once this analysis is complete, I ask students to write their own essays in response to the prompt. While they are crafting these sample answers for a timed writing test, I do not ask them to write those texts in a timed setting. Instead, I allow time for prewriting, collaboration, and revision, so that students have an opportunity to explore what could go into these test responses under the best writing conditions. This technique allows students to concentrate on learning how to analyze and respond to the prompt, instead of worrying about the time frame. Essentially, I am narrowing the challenges of the assignment so that I can break down the requirements of responding to the test prompt. When they finish their texts, students return to the outlines of their writing processes and make any revisions necessary to better represent the ways that they compose.

Prompt Analysis Chart	
Audience ■ Who are you writing for? ■ What does your reader know about the topic? ■ What opinions does your reader already have about the issue?	
Purpose & Content ■ What are you communicating? ■ What does the prompt ask you to do? ■ What key information should be included?	
Organization & Genre ■ What organizational words does the prompt use? ■ What structure do the words indicate you should use? ■ What genre will your essay use?	
Personal Expertise ■ What do you know about the topic or issue? ■ What personal expertise can you share with your reader? ■ What do you know about the topic that your reader doesn't know?	
Designing Writing Assignments by Traci Gardner ©2008 National Council of Teachers of English.	

Figure 5.1. Students can fill out this prompt and explore a task in a structured way.

Providing Support and Explanatory Materials

Designing supporting materials for an unknown assignment is quite a challenge. My solution has been to focus on supporting students' processes and writing strategies, since I cannot provide specific resources for the actual prompt. I ask students to review all their notes on test writing and choose an image that represents their own writing abilities, providing this prompt:

> Describe yourself as a test writer by using an analogy. Begin by completing this sentence: "When I write a timed essay, I am like a _____." For example, you might complete the sentence this way: "When I write a timed essay, I am like a gardener." After you've come up with your analogy, explore your choice in a journal entry. If I were comparing myself to a gardener, I'd talk about the way that I get started on a paper and the way that I start work on a garden—gathering seeds and tools is like gathering ideas and basic information about the writing prompt. Your response should do two things: show how you write a timed essay and make comparisons that clarify for your readers the way that you write.

Once they've written their analogies, I have students share their ideas in small groups or with the whole class, asking them to note things that they have discovered about themselves as writers as a result of this self-analysis. Additionally, I encourage students to compare the strategies they use during timed essays with those they use during other writing situations.

As time draws closer to the date of the actual timed test, I set aside a class period for students to draw conclusions about strategies to ensure they do their best work on the test. Students look over all the work we've completed on timed writing—journal entries, notes, their responses to samples, and so on—and then choose five tips for writing an essay for a standardized test. Additionally, students explain briefly why they've chosen each tip. Working in small groups once they finish, students share their tips and create a group list of the eight to ten best pieces of advice. Groups then share their lists and the justification for their choices with the whole class. These group lists go up in the classroom for students to refer to in the days leading up to the test.

Finally, I ask students to construct a mental writing kit. I cannot send them to take standardized tests with notes and analysis charts, but I can outfit them with mental tools that they can rely on as they write.

Using all the information that they have gathered, students create their own writing kit composed of tips, plans, and key structures that they can tap as they work, as described in the following prompt:

> Think about the things that come in a kit that you're familiar with (for instance, a first aid kit, a sewing kit, a bicycle repair kit, or a starter kit for DSL). The kit includes supplies, tools, and instructions. Your task is to design your own kit for standardized test writing. Since you cannot take any tools into the test itself, your writing kit must consist of mental tools, such as tips, plans, and organizational structures. Think about the process that you use when you write on standardized tests and what you know about the kind of writing that is required and then create your own personal list of supplies that you'll plan to use on test day. In your journal, list the items you'd include and then compose the instruction booklet that would accompany the items.

I emphasize that everyone's writing kit will include different items, since the tools that each person needs are different. One student's test writing kit included the following items:

- Prompt Analysis Questions: Who? Why? Expertise?
- Read—Circle Words—Jot Notes—Write—Edit
- Close eyes and refocus when distracted
- *A/an* for count and *the* for noncount
- Begin with attention-getter and end with "So what?"

In her writing kit, this student included several different kinds of tools. The first and second items are essentially prewriting tools that she used to define the task she was to complete and plan the writing she would do in response. Worried about running out of time, she added the third item, "Close eyes and refocus when distracted," which is a simple strategy to ensure that she stays on task as she writes her test essay. As a student who spoke Chinese as her first language, she noted in her fourth item a reminder for the pesky article rules that English uses. Finally, she included a note on the desired structure for her essay.

If there are any special features of the test that students are preparing for, I talk about how those aspects might influence the items in the writers' kits. For instance, if the test includes a page for notes, I talk about how students can jot the items from their kits on that sheet when they begin work on the timed essays. As another example, if students are allowed to write in the test booklets, I might suggest circling key words in the essay prompt as an analysis tool they can include in their kits.

Because students need to remember the items in their kits, I have them present their tools to one another orally and without notes. As part of their discussion, I ask students to examine how the tools might change if they were doing a different kind of writing. When the kits are ready, I have students test them out by completing another sample response to a test prompt, this one in a timed setting. After they've finished writing, I ask them to reevaluate their kits to assess how well the tools worked.

6 More Writing Assignment Resources

These texts include nice explanations and examples of how to design effective writing assignments:

- *The St. Martin's Guide to Teaching Writing* (5th ed.) by Cheryl Glenn, Melissa A. Goldwaithe, and Robert Conners (2003)
- *A Rhetoric for Writing Teachers* (4th ed.) by Erika Lindemann with Daniel Anderson (2001)
- *Both Art and Craft: Teaching Ideas That Spark Learning* by Diana Mitchell and Leila Christenbury (2000)
- *Assigning, Responding, Evaluating: A Writing Teacher's Guide* (3rd ed.) by Edward M. White (1999)

For more details on unpacking the language of writing assignments, see Jim Burke's "Learning the Language of Academic Study" from the May 2004 issue of *Voices from the Middle* (pp. 37–42). For a collection of topics that students can focus their texts on, get a copy of *What Can I Write About? 7,000 Topics for High School Students* (2002). You can use the basic topics listed in this book as starting points for assignments that you design.

Online resources on writing assignments are available on a companion website: http://www.ncte.org/books/10850/. This site includes the following materials:

- links to relevant NCTE standards, position statements, and guidelines
- an annotated bibliography of the works cited in this text, including links to NCTE journal articles that allow subscribers to read more about any topic easily
- links to ReadWriteThink lesson plans related to the examples in this text, which have been marked by this "Lesson Plan" icon:
- links to additional teaching resources and lesson plans that focus on writing assignments
- reproducible copies of the example assignment prompts and charts included in this text

Sample Starting Points for Writing Assignments

The remainder of this chapter lists writing prompts, arranged by writing type, that you can customize for the classes that you teach. These prompts, of course, are only starting points, similar to those included in Chapter 4. Once you find one that you want to use, work it into a complete assignment by adding the details and resources that define the task for your students, explore the related expectations, and provide supporting materials. Be sure that you shape the audience and purpose and supply the related resources necessary for an effective writing assignment geared toward your students.

Narrative

Being Unprepared. Because you have been sick, out of town, busy at work, or finishing other homework, you didn't have as much time as you needed to study for an important test. Everyone going to school has been in this situation. Think of a specific test that you took that you felt unprepared for and narrate the events surrounding it. Tell your readers about the preparation that you were able to do, the reasons that you didn't get to prepare as well as you wanted, the test itself, and any significant events that happened after you took it. Your paper should help readers understand what it felt like to be unprepared.

Light Bulb Moment. Think of a time when you realized that you suddenly understood an idea, a skill, or a concept you had been struggling with—it might be an idea discussed in a class or a specific athletic skill you were trying to perfect. For instance, you might think about when you were trying to understand how to identify iambic pentameter in a poem or how to complete a Taylor Series problem in your calculus class. Or you might consider when you were trying to perfect your free throws and suddenly understood how your follow-through was affecting your success. Write a narrative that tells the story of your movement toward understanding. How did you finally come to understand? What changed your perceptions and gave you a new understanding? Your paper should help readers grasp how you felt when you struggled with the idea or skill and then how you felt at the moment of insight.

Childhood Event. Choose a vivid time from your childhood—you might think of your first ride on a school bus, a visit to the principal's office, the first A you earned on a test or paper, earning money to buy something that you really wanted, and so on. Narrate the events related to the childhood memory that you've chosen so that your readers will understand why the event was important and memorable.

Literature Option. Have students imagine a childhood event for the main character in a piece of literature and connect it to the behavior the character shows in the story.

Achieving a Goal. Think of a time when you achieved a personal goal—you might have finally completed a marathon or triathlon, bettered your score on the SATs, or learned to create your own website. Tell your readers the story of how you met your goal. Be sure that your readers understand why the goal is important to you.

The Good and the Bad. Think about an event in your life that seemed bad but turned out to be good. Maybe you got injured and while you were waiting for your broken leg to heal, you learned how to use a computer. The thing that makes the event change from a bad one to a good one may be something that you learned as a result, something that you did differently as a result, or something that happened that wouldn't have occurred otherwise. Tell the story of the event and help your readers understand how this event that seemed negative turned out to have positive consequences.

Literature Option. As a book report alternative, ask students to consider how a character in a book realizes that an event that originally seemed negative was ultimately a positive influence.

Being a Teacher. Teaching someone else how to do something can be rewarding. Think of a skill that you've taught someone. Perhaps you taught someone how to swim, showed someone how to bake a soufflé, or helped someone learn to study more effectively. Think about the events that made up the process of teaching the skill and narrate the story for your readers.

Changing Places. Every place has things that change—sometimes as the result of economics, sometimes because different people are involved, and sometimes for no clear reason that you know about. Think of a change to a place that you know well. Perhaps Smith and Bros. Grocery, your local grocery store, was bought out by a regional chain like Food Lion or Winn Dixie. Maybe the First National Bank of Smithburg suddenly became CitiBank. Perhaps the change was more personal—an older sibling moved out of the house and your family turned the bedroom into a guest room or an office. Think of a specific change and narrate the events that occurred. Readers should know the details of the change, and they should know how you feel about it.

Personal Rituals. Describe a personal ritual that you, your friends, or your family members have. For example, think about the personal steps that you always go through when you prepare for an exam. Do you sit at a desk, spread books and notes across your bed, or use the kitchen table? Do you have to have something to drink—soda, water, Red Bull? We do numerous things for which we create personal rituals. Choose one event—studying for a test, writing a paper, dressing and warming up before a game, or preparing and having a special family meal. Narrate the events that take place when you complete your ritual so that your readers understand the steps that the ritual includes and why you complete them.

Standing Up. Choose a time when you did something that took a lot of nerve, a time when you didn't follow the crowd, or a time when you stood up for your beliefs. Perhaps your friends were urging you to do something that you were uncomfortable with and you chose not to cave to peer pressure. Maybe you took a stance on a political issue that was important in your community. Whatever experience you choose, think about the details of the event and write a story that tells what happened. Show your readers why you decided to make a stand or try something that took nerve, give specifics on the event, and share how you felt after the event.

Disagreeing. Think of a time when you disagreed with a decision that had been made and did something about it. The decision might have been made by someone you know personally—your biology teacher announced a new policy to grade for spelling and grammar on your quizzes and homework or an older family member decided to cancel a subscription to a magazine that you liked to read or an online service that you liked to use. You might have responded by discussing your concerns with your principal or dean, or you might have decided to get a part-time job to earn enough money to buy the magazine yourself. Or the decision could have been made by someone you never met— perhaps your school board decided to change the boundary lines in your school district so that you would have to go to a different school, or your state legislature passed a bill that you disagreed with. Your response might have been to write a letter to the editor, to your state representative, or to the school board. Whatever happened, your job now is to write a paper that narrates the events that occurred—from the decision that was made to your response. Be sure to include enough details so that your readers understand why you disagreed with the decision and why you felt that your response was appropriate.

Informative

New Policies. Your school has instituted some new policies. Most students seem to understand the rules, but not everyone is aware of the reasons for the policies or the specific details. Your school's administration has decided that the best way to deal with the situation is to create a handbook that explains all the school's rules and guidelines. The handbook will be distributed to all students this year, and it will become an ongoing piece of the new orientation packet given to new students each fall. Your job is to choose one of the new policies and write an explanation that tells readers what it is, the reason it exists, and what happens if it is broken.

Definition. A local civic organization is having a scholarship contest for students at your school. The winner will get a $1,500 prize. To enter, you have to write an essay that answers the question "What Is a Student at [Your School]?" or "What Does *Education* Mean at [Your School]?" Your job is to define the term "Student" or "Education" in the context of your school. Be sure to include concrete examples and details to support your definition.

Note. Customize the assignment by replacing "[Your School]" with the name of your own school (e.g., "What Is a Student at Thomas Dale High School?").

Literature Option. For a piece of literature that includes a school or educational setting, ask students to write from the perspective of a character in the book, adapting the assignment to fit the text. For instance, a student might adopt the character of Holden Caufield and write a journal or diary entry that focuses on the question "What Does *Education* Mean at Pencey Prep?"

Biography. To help students and parents learn more about the people working at your school, your school's website is featuring a biography of a new staff member each day. The goal of this part of the website is to share information about the staff so that everyone knows more about the people that students interact with daily. Your job is to choose a staff member and write his or her biographical statement. Think about the kinds of things that families and students probably want to know about the people who work at your school—and remember that other staff members will read the biographical statements too. You'll write two pieces: a twenty-five-word blurb for the homepage and a longer profile (about two double-spaced pages) with more information. There will be a "MORE. . ." link at the end of the short blurb on the homepage that will lead to the second profile.

Literature Option. Have students construct a similar website composed of biographical statements for characters in a piece of literature. The biographies might focus on faculty and students at a school, members of a community organization, or people in a workplace. Students could also focus simply on characters in a book, creating biographies appropriate for a guide to that work. This activity can be a useful review activity and creates an artifact that students can return to as they study for semester examinations.

Newspaper Story. Write an announcement for your local newspaper about an upcoming event at your school, your local community center, a nearby religious center, or a similar location. Provide details on the event so that readers will learn everything they need to know in order to attend: Why is the event going on? Who is organizing it? Who can attend? When will it happen? What special information can you share about the event? Be sure that your writing not only provides the details but also does so in a way that will entice readers to participate.

PSA. Celebrate a special month by creating a public service announcement for your morning intercom announcements or for public access TV or radio. Consult a calendar to choose an existing celebration (e.g., Black History Month in February) or select a special group or topic, such as famous people from your state or important scientific discoveries, to honor in your month-long celebration. Prepare an announcement for each day, highlighting a different person or achievement. The announcement should provide all the basic details on the subject and indicate why the person or achievement was significant. If resources at your school do not allow for schoolwide announcements, consider beginning each class period with an announcement. Compile printed copies of the announcements in a class anthology or bulletin board so that other students can revisit the information.

Field Trip. Your class or a club you are a member of is preparing for a field trip to a local point of interest. Everyone in the class or club has chosen a different location to explore. Each of you is to write a short description of the location you've chosen. All of the descriptions will be shared so that your group can choose where to go. You need to include everything about the location: hours, cost, features, any special events, and so forth. Your job is not to persuade your class or club to choose your location. You're simply to provide a fair, informative description of the location so that all the places your group can visit can be evaluated.

Literature Option. As preparation for a piece of literature that follows characters as they travel, ask students to investigate and report on specific places that the characters are likely to encounter. You might choose specific places mentioned in the work or locations in the cities or towns mentioned in it. Depending upon the piece of literature, students might research the location as it currently is or as it would have been in the time when the piece of literature is set.

Tradition. Explain a tradition to someone who is not familiar with the custom. It can be a tradition for your family, within your community, related to your religious beliefs, or practiced by members of a club that you belong to. Imagine that someone is coming to an event where the tradition will be prominent or that someone will participate in the tradition. Your job is to write that person a letter or an email message explaining the tradition. Include details on what happens, when it happens, why it happens, and so forth. Give the reader everything he or she will need to participate in or understand your tradition.

Literature Option. Choose a tradition that is included in a piece of literature and ask students to write a letter to someone who will join in on the tradition in the future. If relevant, students can do outside research to complement the information included in the text.

Calendar. Create a school calendar for your website, marking vacation dates, important deadlines, sporting events, and so forth. Each brief entry should explain the significance of the date, listing any special information about time and location as well as including background details and links to any additional resources. Begin by brainstorming a list of major school events that occur over the course of the year (e.g., special social events, homecoming week activities, debate competitions, dramatic performances, and graduation) and their significance.

Note. This can be an assignment that students create one year to leave behind for students who come the next year, or it can be a rolling assignment, with different students adding to the calendar each month.

Influential Object. Write an essay about an object in the school that has influenced you in an important way this year. You may write about something you own or use on a regular basis (a book, a picture in your locker, or a gym uniform) or an object that you interact with only occasionally (the unabridged dictionary in the library). The object that you choose should be one that you could hold: choose a book in the library rather than the whole library, for instance. Explain specific ways that this object has influenced you. Support your ideas with examples and details. All the responses will be collected and shared with new students who come to the school.

Note. Customize this prompt to fit your situation. For instance, if you're working with first-year college students, the last sentence can explain that the responses will be shared with incoming first-year students next fall.

Literature Option. Have students choose the most influential object for a character in a text and write a similar essay that explains why the object is so important to the character. Students can write in the voice of the character or in their own voices, as observers of the character's behavior.

Biggest Myth. What is the biggest myth about the ninth grade? Write a letter to the editor of your school paper or for a collection to be shared with new students in the fall that explains the biggest falsehood you were told when you were an eighth grader. In your letter, be sure to describe what you heard before you came to the school and then reveal the truth about the situation. Add details that suggest why the myth has developed. Your goal is to create a myth-busting resource for students who will be in your position next year.

Note. Customize this prompt to fit your situation. For instance, you might ask students to write on the biggest myth about American literature class. Additionally, you might allow students to focus their work further (e.g., the biggest myth about being in the marching band rather than about the ninth grade).

Literature Option. Ask students to write from the perspective of a character in a piece of literature and explain the biggest myth from that character's perspective. For instance, students might write "The Biggest Myth about Being Rich" by Jay Gatsby or "The Biggest Myth about the English Language" by Eliza Doolittle.

Analysis

Naming. Take a close look at the names that are used for events, people, and things that are associated with a specific current event or controversial issue. In relation to military activities, for instance, think about who uses the word "war" and who uses other names. Consider the connotations and the denotations of the words used. Choose several related terms that are being used. In your paper, analyze this diction. What is the purpose of such names? What audience are they pointed toward? What tone does the writer want to communicate to readers/listeners? What conclusions can you draw about the writer's rhetorical strategies?

Note. Here are some loaded terms used in wars over the last few decades: *ethnic cleansing, peacekeepers, police action, death squad, insurgents,* and *freedom fighters*. Use these terms to demonstrate the analysis that students will do for the topic that they choose.

Literature Option. Ask students to consider the names used for events, people, and things in a piece of literature. Students might trace all the names associated with a specific character and draw conclusions about the relationships among characters based on the names, or they could consider how the different names for a particular group or event communicate underlying values that influence the text. Demonstrate the possibilities by using the various names for the character Voldemort from the Harry Potter series.

Evasion. Choose a speech or statement of a group involved in a specific current event or controversial issue. Be sure that you find a specific statement by the group rather than paraphrased statements—the group's website will probably have texts that you can use. Look closely at what the group's representative says in the speech or statement and then step back and think of all the things that are *not* said. What issues has the writer avoided? What descriptions are missing? Which people are never mentioned? Who never speaks? What emotions are not dealt with? Write a paper that explains the absences in the text. Account for the writer's rhetorical purpose in avoiding these issues.

Note. For a connection to history or to the setting of a piece of literature, choose historical speeches that fit the time period rather than contemporary statements.

Objective vs. Subjective. Focus on a news broadcast, a newspaper or magazine article, a news briefing, or another speech or statement available online, in print, on the radio, or on television. Go through the text and separate the objective details and material from the subjective details and material. When does the writer use objective details, and when does the writer rely on subjective details? Write text that analyzes the ways that the writer uses these different kinds of details.

Literature Option. Have students complete a similar search but use a piece of literature instead. For instance, students might separate the objective and subjective statements in the play *Inherit the Wind* or in the short story "A Jury of Her Peers."

Firsthand Reports. Compare firsthand reports for two or more similar events (e.g., natural disasters, centennial celebrations, Super Bowl games). Look at what the writer or speaker says, the things that are described, the emotions that are expressed, and the explanations for events that are given. You might even test yourself and your friends: if you remove place names and other obvious identifying information, can you tell which event the firsthand report refers to? Write a comparison/ contrast paper that explores the relationships between the reports and accounts for the reasons that the firsthand reports echo or diverge from each other.

Literature Option. If the class is reading a text that includes firsthand reports, such as *Nothing but the Truth* by Avi, ask them to complete a similar assignment by focusing on the reports in the text.

Picture This. Examine the ways that pictures, graphics, and films are used to communicate information about a specific current event or controversial issue on three different websites. What role do these media fill? What rhetorical purpose do they serve? How do they relate to words about them—Is there an audio recording that plays? Are words included in a sidebar or caption? Is there any music or sound effect related to the pictures, graphics, or film? How do the parameters change by author and by audience for the sites? For example, how are the pictures that are used in a government briefing different from those used on the evening news, shown on a newspaper website, or provided on a relief agency's website? Create a classification system that accounts for the kinds of pictures, graphics, and films that are used, when they are used, and the ways that they are used.

Role of Television. Edward R. Murrow said, "Television in the main is being used to distract, delude, amuse, and insulate us." In light of Murrow's quotation, what role would you say that television plays in a specific current event or controversial issue? Does television distract? If so, from what, and how? Or does it delude? Who is being deluded? What methods does television use to do this? If television amuses, whom does it amuse, and what techniques are used? If television is insulating us, what is it insulating us from, and how are we being insulated? Does television fill several roles? Or do you see the media as filling roles that Murrow has not allowed for? Explain the general roles that television fills, but focus on specific television coverage and provide examples and explanations from the shows that support your analysis.

Gender and Violence. Analyze the ways that gender plays a role in discussions of violence and in portrayals of violent actions on television, in movies, in video games, and in other media. How often do the discussions focus on men/boys and women/girls, and how often do they refer to people generally? When is the gender specified—and more importantly, why? How do stereotypes influence the portrayals, and how do the portrayals create (or support) stereotypes? Choose one show, movie, game, or website to focus on and analyze the ways that gender and violence are connected (or not) in its presentation of information. In your paper, consider the specific roles/characters involved, their actions and interactions, and the underlying messages that the television show, movie, game, or article is sending to viewers, readers, or players.

Persuasion

Litter. A litter problem has developed on your school's campus. Students are throwing trash on the ground, leaving empty soda cans and bottles outside on the benches, and dropping napkins and other trash on the cafeteria floor instead of carrying them to the trash can. Your principal asked students to take more care, but the litter problem persisted. The principal has reacted by canceling all extracurricular activities until students consistently clean up after themselves. What is your position on the issue? Write a letter to the editor of the school newspaper in support of or against the principal's solution.

New Highway Exit. The state has created a plan to add a second highway exit to help shoppers access a busy mall. The only problem is that the new exit will move the access road 500 yards closer to a nearby elementary school. Teachers and parents at the school complain that moving the road closer will increase noise at the school and provide unnecessary distractions. The state plans to include privacy fences to help solve the problems, but protesters are unsatisfied. Write a letter outlining your position to the local school board or the state planners and support your view with convincing reasons.

Computers in the Classroom. As part of a new technology initiative, your local school district is increasing the number of computers in every school. The district plan provides for two computers in every classroom. Teachers at your school are lobbying instead to place all the computers together to create two computer-based classrooms so that all students in a class, rather than only one or two students, can work at the computers at once. The district is worried about the additional cost of creating and maintaining these special classrooms and is concerned about how access to the classrooms can be provided fairly and efficiently. What is your position on this issue? Write a persuasive letter asking the local school board to adopt your point of view on how the computers should be set up.

Endorsement. Write a letter of endorsement (or an endorsement speech) for a political candidate, referendum initiative, or similar item on your local election ballot. In your letter, state which candidate or position you support and provide a complete explanation for the reasons that you've chosen your position. Remember that the information in your letter needs to convince readers or listeners that you've thought about the issues involved and have concrete reasons for the choice that you've made.

Ask a School Visitor. Several students will be allowed to ask a question of an important visitor who is coming to your school. The school's administration has devised a contest to choose the lucky students. To enter the contest, you have to write the question you want to ask as well as a justification for the question that explains why the issue is important to other students and why it matters to you. Entries are limited to one typed page. The visitor will read the winning entries before the debate, so the background information that you provide will help the visitor understand the purpose of your question. The administrators will select the winner on the basis of the originality of the question, whether others would be interested in the question, and the persuasiveness of the explanation. Write your entry for the contest.

Note. Be sure to choose a specific speaker for this activity so that students can focus their entries.

Literature Option. Have students propose questions for a literary character from a text the class is familiar with.

Literary Analysis

Breaking News. Choose a critical event from your reading and write a news brief on the events to be videotaped or posted on a news website.

Note. Update the story, if desired, for the medium. For instance, students can discuss the differences between a news report written on the events in *The Scarlet Letter* today and one that would have been included in a bulletin distributed at the time. Add a twist to the assignment by having students choose the website where the story will be posted (e.g., a cable news site, an entertainment site, a gossip site).

Advice Letter. Assume the role of a character from a story you have read and write a letter to an advice columnist to ask for suggestions on how to handle a particular problem that the character faces. Be sure to include details about the challenge that make the situation clear to the columnist. Next, take the role of the advice columnist and respond to the letter by addressing the challenge that the character has identified.

Note. A great strategy when students have all read the same text is to have students exchange the character letters and respond to those letters, instead of their own, as the advice columnist.

Missing Scene. Have students choose a scene that isn't included in a reading and write their versions of the events that might happen. Students can concentrate on events that are referred to but aren't explored, or they can focus on a time period that passes without comment.

What happened the night before the events that open *A Raisin in the Sun,* for instance? Describe a scene from either Othello's or Desdemona's childhood—that is, before they met. What happened before Mr. Mallard went to work in "The Story of an Hour"?

Characters in the Future. Where will the characters be in twenty years? Choose one character and use the information in the text to imagine his or her future. Once you think through the character's future, write a narrative, a letter to another character, or an address at a twenty-year reunion.

Opposites Attract. You've probably heard the phrase "opposites attract." You may even have studied the principle in a science class. For your assignment, think about the ways that the notion applies (or doesn't) to the foil and main characters in a play or other piece of literature. In what ways do their opposite characteristics, values, and behaviors bring them closer together instead of separating them? Are they in some ways different halves of the same whole? Explore the connections that bind them while establishing their contrast—and move beyond the basics of their relationship to address the ways that their opposition and attraction affect the text.

Diary Entry. Choose a particularly involved exchange between two characters in the reading—they may have had an argument, one may have confessed something to the other, or perhaps they just had a long sharing of beliefs. Take on the persona of one character. Imagine that you, as the character, go back to your room (or home or office or whatever makes sense) and get out your personal diary. Now write your private, personal account of the interaction. Include not just what happened but also your personal reaction to the events and any motivation for your reaction. Naturally, whatever you said to the other character may not be identical to the thoughts that went through your head. Here in your diary, you're confessing all! What did you think? What did you say? And what were your motivations during the discussion? *Note.* Once students finish the diary entries for one character, have them step back into the other character's persona and write entries from that point of view. When they finish, ask them to reflect on how they chose the motivations and reactions that the characters had.

Appendix: NCTE Beliefs about the Teaching of Writing

The Writing Study Group of the NCTE Executive Committee
November 2004

Just as the nature of and expectation for literacy has changed in the past century and a half, so has the nature of writing. Much of that change has been due to technological developments, from pen and paper, to typewriter, to word processor, to networked computer, to design software capable of composing words, images, and sounds. These developments not only expanded the types of texts that writers produce, they also expanded immediate access to a wider variety of readers. With full recognition that writing is an increasingly multifaceted activity, we offer several principles that should guide effective teaching practice.

1. Everyone has the capacity to write, writing can be taught, and teachers can help students become better writers.

Though poets and novelists may enjoy debating whether or not writing can be taught, teachers of writing have more pragmatic aims. Setting aside the question of whether one can learn to be an artistic genius, there is ample empirical evidence that anyone can get better at writing, and that what teachers do makes a difference in how much students are capable of achieving as writers.

Developing writers require support. This support can best come through carefully designed writing instruction oriented toward acquiring new strategies and skills. Certainly, writers can benefit from teachers who simply support and give them time to write. However, instruction matters. Teachers of writing should be well-versed in composition theory and research, and they should know methods for turning that theory into practice. When writing teachers first walk into classrooms, they should already know and practice good composition. However, much as in doctoring, learning to teach well is a lifetime process, and lifetime professional development is the key to successful practice. Students deserve no less.

2. People learn to write by writing.

As is the case with many other things people do, getting better at writing requires doing it—a lot. This means actual writing, not merely listening to lectures about writing, doing grammar drills, or discussing readings. The more people write, the easier it gets and the more they are motivated to do it. Writers who write a lot learn more about the process because they have had more experience inside it. Writers learn from each session with their hands on a keyboard or around a pencil as they draft, rethink, revise, and draft again. Thinking about how to make your writing better is what revision is. In other words, improvement is built into the experience of writing.

What does this mean for teaching?

Writing instruction must include ample in-class and out-of-class opportunities for writing and should include writing for a variety of purposes and audiences.

Writing, though, should not be viewed as an activity that happens only within a classroom's walls. Teachers need to support students in the development of writing lives, habits, and preferences for life outside school. We already know that many students do extensive amounts of self-sponsored writing: emailing, keeping journals or doing creative projects, instant messaging, making Web sites, blogging and so on. As much as possible, instruction should be geared toward making sense in a life outside of school, so that writing has ample room to grow in individuals' lives. It is useful for teachers to consider what elements of their curriculum they could imagine students self-sponsoring outside of school. Ultimately, those are the activities that will produce more writing.

In order to provide quality opportunities for student writing, teachers must minimally understand:

- How to interpret curriculum documents, including things that can be taught while students are actually writing, rather than one thing at a time to all students at once.
- The elements of "writing lives" as people construct them in the world outside of school.
- Social structures that support independent work.
- How to confer with individual writers.
- How to assess while students are writing.
- How to plan what students need to know in response to ongoing research.

- How to create a sense of personal safety in the classroom, so that students are willing to write freely and at length.
- How to create community while students are writing in the same room together.

3. Writing is a process.

Often, when people think of writing, they think of texts—finished pieces of writing. Understanding what writers do, however, involves thinking not just about what texts look like when they are finished but also about what strategies writers might employ to produce those texts. Knowledge about writing is only complete with understanding the complex of actions in which writers engage as they produce texts. Such understanding has two aspects. First is the development, through extended practice over years, of a repertory of routines, skills, strategies, and practices, for generating, revising, and editing different kinds of texts. Second is the development of reflective abilities and meta-awareness about writing. This procedural understanding helps writers most when they encounter difficulty, or when they are in the middle of creating a piece of writing. How does someone get started? What do they do when they get stuck? How do they plan the overall process, each section of their work, and even the rest of the sentence they are writing right now? Research, theory, and practice over the past 40 years has produced a richer understanding of what writers do—those who are proficient and professional as well as those who struggle.

Two further points are vital. To say that writing is a process is decidedly not to say that it should—or can—be turned into a formulaic set of steps. Experienced writers shift between different operations according to tasks and circumstances. Second, writers do not accumulate process skills and strategies once and for all. They develop and refine writing skills throughout their writing lives.

What does this mean for teaching?

Whenever possible, teachers should attend to the process that students might follow to produce texts—and not only specify criteria for evaluating finished products, in form or content. Students should become comfortable with pre-writing techniques, multiple strategies for developing and organizing a message, a variety of strategies for revising and editing, and strategies for preparing products for public audiences and for deadlines. In explaining assignments, teachers should provide guidance and options for ways of going about it. Sometimes, evaluating the processes students follow—the decisions they make, the attempts along the way—can be as important as evaluating the final product. At least some of the time, the teacher should guide the students through the process, assisting them as they go. Writing instruction must provide opportunities for students to identify the processes that work best for themselves as they move from one writing situation to another.

Writing instruction must also take into account that a good deal of workplace writing and other writing takes place in collaborative situations. Writers must learn to work effectively with one another.

Teachers need to understand at least the following in order to be excellent at teaching writing as a process:

- The relationship between features of finished writing and the actions writers perform.
- What writers of different genres say about their craft.
- The process of writing from the inside, that is, what they themselves as writers experience in a host of different writing situations.
- Multiple strategies for approaching a wide range of typical problems writers face during composing, including strategies for audience and task analysis, invention, revision, and editing.
- Multiple models of the writing process, the varied ways individuals approach similar tasks, and the ways that writing situations and genres inform processes.
- Published texts, immediately available, that demonstrate a wide range of writing strategies and elements of craft.
- The relationships among the writing process, curriculum, learning, and pedagogy.
- How to design time for students to do their best work on an assignment.
- How writers use tools, including word-processing and design software and computer-based resources.

4. Writing is a tool for thinking.

When writers actually write, they think of things that they did not have in mind before they began writing. The act of writing generates ideas. This is different from the way we often think of writers—as getting ideas fixed in their heads before they write them down. The notion that writing is a medium for thought is important in several ways. It suggests a number of important uses for writing: to solve problems, to identify issues, to construct questions, to reconsider something one had already figured out, to try out a half-baked idea. This insight that writing is a tool for thinking helps us to understand the process of drafting and revision as one of exploration and discovery, and is nothing like transcribing from pre-recorded tape. The writing process is not one of simply fixing up the mistakes in an early draft, but of finding more and more wrinkles and implications in what one is talking about.

What does this mean for teaching?

In any writing classroom, some of the writing is for others and some of the writing is for the writer. Regardless of the age, ability, or experience of the writer, the use of writing to generate thought is still valuable; therefore, forms of writing such as personal narrative, journals, written reflections, observations, and writing-to-learn strategies are important.

In any writing assignment, it must be assumed that part of the work of writers will involve generating and regenerating ideas prior to writing them.

Excellence in teaching writing as thinking requires that the teacher understand:

- Varied tools for thinking through writing, such as journals, writers' notebooks, blogs, sketchbooks, digital portfolios, listservs or online discussion groups, dialogue journals, double-entry or dialectical journals, and others.
- The kinds of new thinking that occur when writers revise.
- The variety of types of thinking people do when they compose, and what those types of thinking look like when they appear in writing.
- Strategies for getting started with an idea, or finding an idea when one does not occur immediately.

5. Writing grows out of many different purposes.

Purposes for writing include developing social networks; engaging in civic discourse; supporting personal and spiritual growth; reflecting on experience; communicating professionally and academically; building relationships with others, including friends, family, and like-minded individuals; and engaging in aesthetic experiences.

Writing is not just one thing. It varies in form, structure, and production process according to its audience and purpose. A note to a cousin is not like a business report, which is different again from a poem. The processes and ways of thinking that lead up to these varied kinds of texts can also vary widely, from the quick single draft email to a friend to the careful drafting and redrafting of a legal contract. The different purposes and forms both grow out of and create various relationships between the writer and the potential reader, and relationships reflected in degrees of formality in language, as well as assumptions about what knowledge and experience is already shared, and what needs to be explained. Writing with certain purposes in mind, the writer focuses her attention on what the audience is thinking or believing; other times, the writer focuses more on the information she is organizing, or on her own thoughts and feelings. Therefore, the thinking, the procedures, and the physical format in writing all differ when writers' purposes vary.

What does this mean for teaching?

Often, in school, students write only to prove that they did something they were asked to do, in order to get credit for it. Or, students are taught a single type of writing and are led to believe this type will suffice in all situations. Writers outside of school have many different purposes beyond demonstrating accountability, and they practice myriad types and genres. In order to make sure students are learning how writing differs when the purpose and the audience differ, it is important that teachers create opportunities for students to be in different kinds of writing situations, where the relationships and agendas are varied. Even within academic settings, the characteristics of good writing vary among disciplines; what counts as a successful lab report, for example, differs from a successful history paper, essay exam, or literary interpretation.

In order to teach for excellence about purposes in writing, teachers need to understand:

- The wide range of purposes for which people write, and the forms of writing that arise from those purposes.
- Strategies and forms for writing for public participation in a democratic society.
- Ways people use writing for personal growth, expression, and reflection and how to encourage and develop this kind of writing.
- Aesthetic or artistic forms of writing and how they are made. That is, the production of creative and literary texts, for the purposes of entertainment, pleasure, or exploration.
- Appropriate forms for varied academic disciplines and the purposes and relationships that create those forms.
- Ways of organizing and transforming school curricula in order to provide students with adequate education in varied purposes for writing.
- How to set up a course to write for varied purposes and audiences.

6. Conventions of finished and edited texts are important to readers and therefore to writers.

Readers expect writing to conform to their expectations, to match the conventions generally established for public texts. Contemporary readers expect words to be spelled in a standardized way, for punctuation to be used in predictable ways, for usage and syntax to match that used in texts they already acknowledge as successful. They expect the style in a piece of writing to be appropriate to its genre and social situation. In other words, it is important that writing that goes public be "correct."

What does this mean for teaching?

Every teacher has to resolve a tension between writing as generating and shaping ideas and writing as demonstrating expected surface conventions. On the one hand, it is important for writing to be as correct as possible and for students to be able to produce correct texts. On the other hand, achieving correctness is only one set of things writers must be able to do; a correct text empty of ideas or unsuited to its audience or purpose is not a good piece of writing. There is no formula for resolving this tension. Writing is both/and: both fluency and fitting conventions. Research shows that facility in these two operations often develops unevenly. For example, as students learn increasingly sophisticated ways of thinking (for example, conditional or subordinate reasoning) or dealing with unfamiliar content, they may produce more surface errors, or perhaps even seem to regress. This is because their mental energies are focused on the new intellectual challenges. Such uneven development is to be tolerated, in fact, encouraged. It is rather like strength gains from lifting weight, which actually tears down muscle fibers only to stimulate them to grow back stronger. Too much emphasis on correctness can actually inhibit development. By the same token, without mastering conventions for written discourse, writers' efforts may come to naught. Drawing readers' attention to the gap between the text at hand and the qualities of texts they expect causes readers to not attend to the content. Each teacher must be knowledgeable enough about the entire landscape of writing instruction to guide particular students toward a goal, developing both increasing fluency in new contexts and mastery of conventions. NCTE's stated policy over many years has been that conventions of writing are best taught in the context of writing. Simply completing workbook or online exercises is inadequate if students are not regularly producing meaningful texts themselves.

Most writing teachers teach students how to edit their writing that will go out to audiences. This is often considered a late stage in the process of composing, because editing is only essential for the words that are left after all the cutting, replacing, rewriting, and adding that go on during revision. Writers need an image in their minds of conventional grammar, spelling, and punctuation in order to compare what is already on the page to an ideal of correctness. They also need to be aware of stylistic options that will produce the most desirable impression on their readers. All of the dimensions of editing are motivated by a concern for an audience.

Teachers should be familiar with techniques for teaching editing and encouraging reflective knowledge about editing conventions. For example, some find it useful to have students review a collection of their writing over time—a journal, notebook, folder, or portfolio—to study empirically the way their writing has changed or needs to change, with respect to conventions. A teacher might say, "let's look at all the times you used commas," or "investigate the ways you might have combined sentences." Such reflective appointments permit students to set goals for their own improvement.

Teachers need to understand at least the following in order to be excellent at teaching conventions to writers:

- Research on developmental factors in writing ability, including the tension between fluency with new operations or contents and the practice of accepted spelling, punctuation, syntactic, and usage conventions.

- The diverse influences and constraints on writers' decision making as they determine the kinds of conventions that apply to this situation and this piece of writing.

- A variety of applications and options for most conventions.

- The appropriate conventions for academic classroom English.

- How to teach usage without excessive linguistic terminology.

- The linguistic terminology that is necessary for teaching particular kinds of usage.

- The linguistic terminology necessary for communicating professionally with other educators.

- The relationship among rhetorical considerations and decisions about conventions, for example, the conditions under which a dash, a comma, a semi-colon, or a full stop might be more effective.

- Conventions beyond the sentence, such as effective uses of bulleted lists, mixed genres and voices, diagrams and charts, design of pages, and composition of video shots.

- An understanding of the relationship among conventions in primary and secondary discourses.
- The conditions under which people learn to do new things with language.
- The relationship among fluency, clarity, and correctness in writing development and the ability to assess which is the leading edge of the student's learning now.

7. Writing and reading are related.

Writing and reading are related. People who read a lot have a much easier time getting better at writing. In order to write a particular kind of text, it helps if the writer has read that kind of text. In order to take on a particular style of language, the writer needs to have read that language, to have heard it in her mind, so that she can hear it again in order to compose it.

Writing can also help people become better readers. In their earliest writing experiences, children listen for the relationships of sounds to letters, which contributes greatly to their phonemic awareness and phonics knowledge. Writers also must learn how texts are structured, because they have to create them. The experience of plotting a short story, organizing a research report, or making line breaks in a poem permits the writer, as a reader, to approach new reading experiences with more informed eyes.

Additionally, reading is a vital source of information and ideas. For writers fully to contribute to a given topic or to be effective in a given situation, they must be familiar with what previous writers have said. Reading also creates a sense of what one's audience knows or expects on a topic.

What does this mean for teaching?

One way to help students become better writers is to make sure they have lots of extended time to read, in school and out. Most research indicates that the easiest way to tap motivation to read is to teach students to choose books and other texts they understand and enjoy, and then to give them time in school to read them. In addition to making students stronger readers, this practice makes them stronger writers.

Students should also have access to and experience in reading material that presents both published and student writing in various genres. Through immersion in a genre, students develop an internalized sense of why an author would select a particular genre for a particular purpose, the power of a particular genre to convey a message, and the rhetorical constraints and possibilities inherent in a genre. Students should be taught the features of different genres, experientially not only explicitly, so that they develop facilities in producing them and become familiar with variant features. If one is going to write in a genre, it is very helpful to have read in that genre first.

Overall, frequent conversations about the connections between what we read and what we write are helpful. These connections will sometimes be about the structure and craft of the writing itself, and sometimes about thematic and content connections.

In order to do an excellent job of teaching into the connections of writing and reading, teachers need to understand at least these things:

- How writers read in a special way, with an eye toward not just what the text says but how it is put together.

- The psychological and social processes reading and writing have in common.

- The ways writers form and use constructs of their intended readers, anticipating their responses and needs.

- An understanding of text structure that is fluid enough to accommodate frequent disruptions.

8. Writing has a complex relationship to talk.

From its beginnings in early childhood through the most complex setting imaginable, writing exists in a nest of talk. Conversely, speakers usually write notes and, regularly, scripts, and they often prepare visual materials that include texts and images. Writers often talk in order to rehearse the language and content that will go into what they write, and conversation often provides an impetus or occasion for writing. They sometimes confer with teachers and other writers about what to do next, how to improve their drafts, or in order to clarify their ideas and purposes. Their usual ways of speaking sometimes do and sometimes do not feed into the sentences they write, depending on an intricate set of decisions writers make continually. One of the features of writing that is most evident and yet most difficult to discuss is the degree to which it has "voice." The fact that we use this term, even in the absence of actual sound waves, reveals some of the special relationship between speech and writing.

What does this mean for teaching?

In early writing, we can expect lots of talk to surround writing, since what children are doing is figuring out how to get speech onto paper. Early teaching in composition should also attend to helping children get used to producing language orally, through telling stories, explaining how things work, predicting what will happen, and guessing about why things and people are the way they are. Early writing experiences will include students explaining orally what is in a text, whether it is printed or drawn.

As they grow, writers still need opportunities to talk about what they are writing about, to rehearse the language of their upcoming texts and run ideas by trusted colleagues before taking the risk of committing words to paper. After making a draft, it is often helpful for writers to discuss with peers what they have done, partly in order to get ideas from their peers, partly to see what they, the writers, say when they try to explain their thinking. Writing conferences, wherein student writers talk about their work with a teacher, who can make suggestions or reorient what the writer is doing, are also very helpful uses of talk in the writing process.

To take advantage of the strong relationships between talk and writing, teachers must minimally understand:

- Ways of setting up and managing student talk in partnerships and groups.
- Ways of establishing a balance between talk and writing in classroom management.
- Ways of organizing the classroom and/or schedule to permit individual teacher-student conferences.
- Strategies for deliberate insertions of opportunities for talk into the writing process: knowing when and how students should talk about their writing.
- Ways of anticipating and solving interpersonal conflicts that arise when students discuss writing.
- Group dynamics in classrooms.
- Relationships—both similarities and differences—between oral and literate language.
- The uses of writing in public presentations and the values of students making oral presentations that grow out of and use their writing.

9. Literate practices are embedded in complicated social relationships.

Writing happens in the midst of a web of relationships. There is, most obviously, the relationship between the writer and the reader. That relationship is often very specific: writers have a definite idea of who will read their words, not just a generalized notion that their text will be available to the world. Furthermore, particular people surround the writer—other writers, partners in purposes, friends, members of a given community—during the process of composing. They may know what the writer is doing and be indirectly involved in it, though they are not the audience for the work. In workplace and academic settings, writers write because someone in authority tells them to. Therefore, power relationships are built into the writing situation. In every writing situation, the writer, the reader, and all relevant others live in a structured social order, where some people's words count more than others, where being heard is more difficult for some people than others, where some people's words come true and others' do not.

Writers start in different places. It makes a difference what kind of language a writer spoke while growing up, and what kinds of language they are being asked to take on later in their experience. It makes a difference, too, the culture a writer comes from, the ways people use language in that culture and the degree to which that culture is privileged in the larger society. Important cultural differences are not only ethnic but also racial, economic, geographical and ideological. For example, rural students from small communities will have different language experiences than suburban students from comprehensive high schools, and students who come from very conservative backgrounds where certain texts are privileged or excluded will have different language experiences than those from progressive backgrounds where the same is true. How much a writer has access to wide, diverse experiences and means of communication creates predispositions and skill for composing for an audience.

What does this mean for teaching?

The teaching of writing should assume students will begin with the sort of language with which they are most at home and most fluent in their speech. That language may be a dialect of English, or even a different language altogether. The goal is not to leave students where they are, however, but to move them toward greater flexibility, so that they can write not just for their own intimates but for wider audiences. Even as they move toward more widely-used English, it is not necessary or desirable to wipe out the ways their family and neighborhood of origin use words. The teaching of excellence in writing means adding language to what already exists, not subtracting. The goal is to make more relationships available, not fewer.

In order to teach for excellence, a writing teacher needs understandings like these about contexts of language:

- How to find out about students' language use in the home and neighborhoods, the changes in language context they may have encountered in their lives, and the kinds of language they most value.

- That wider social situations in which students write, speak, read, and relate to other people affect what seems "natural" or "easy" to them—or not.

- How to discuss with students the need for flexibility in the employment of different kinds of language for different social contexts.

- How to help students negotiate maintenance of their most familiar language while mastering academic classroom English and the varieties of English used globally.

- Control and awareness of their own varied languages and linguistic contexts.

- An understanding of the relationships among group affiliation, identity, and language.

- Knowledge of the usual patterns of common dialects in English, such as African American English, Spanish and varieties of English related to Spanish, common patterns in American rural and urban populations, predictable patterns in the English varieties of groups common in their teaching contexts.

- How and why to study a community's ways of using language.

10. Composing occurs in different modalities and technologies.

Increasingly rapid changes in technologies mean that composing is involving a combination of modalities, such as print, still images, video, and sound. Computers make it possible for these modalities to combine in the same work environment. Connections to the Internet not only make a range of materials available to writers, they also collapse distances between writers and readers and between generating words and creating designs. Print always has a visual component, even if it is only the arrangement of text on a page and the type font. Furthermore, throughout history, print has often been partnered with pictures in order to convey more meaning, to add attractiveness, and to appeal to a wider audience. Television, video, and film all involve such combinations, as do websites and presentation software. As basic tools for communicating expand to include modes beyond print alone, "writing" comes to mean more than scratching words with pen and paper. Writers need to be able to think about the physical design of text, about the appropriateness and thematic content of visual images, about the integration of sound with a reading experience, and about the medium that is most appropriate for a particular message, purpose, and audience.

What does this mean for teaching?

Writing instruction must accommodate the explosion in technology from the world around us.

From the use of basic word processing to support drafting, revision, and editing to the use of hypertext and the infusion of visual components in writing, the definition of what writing instruction includes must evolve to embrace new requirements.

Many teachers and students do not, however, have adequate access to computing, recording, and video equipment to take advantage of the most up-to-date technologies. In many cases, teaching about the multi-modal nature of writing is best accomplished through varying the forms of writing with more ordinary implements. Writing picture books allows students to think between text and images, considering the ways they work together and distribute the reader's attention. Similar kinds of visual/verbal thinking can be supported through other illustrated text forms, including some kinds of journals/sketchbooks and posters. In addition, writing for performance requires the writer to imagine what the audience will see and hear and thus draws upon multiple modes of thinking, even in the production of a print text. Such uses of technology without the latest equipment reveal the extent to which "new" literacies are rooted also in older ones.

Teachers need to understand at least the following in order to be excellent at teaching composition as involving multiple media:

- A range of new genres that have emerged with the increase in electronic communication. Because these genres are continually evolving, this knowledge must be continually updated.
- Operation of some of the hardware and software their students will use, including resources for solving software and hardware problems.
- Internet resources for remaining up to date on technologies.
- Design principles for Web pages.
- E-mail and chat conventions.
- How to navigate both the World Wide Web and web-based databases.
- The use of software for making Web sites, including basic html, such as how to make a link.
- Theory about the relationship between print and other modalities.

11. Assessment of writing involves complex, informed, human judgment.

Assessment of writing occurs for different purposes. Sometimes, a teacher assesses in order to decide what the student has achieved and what he or she still needs to learn. Sometimes, an entity beyond the classroom assesses a student's level of achievement in order to say whether they can go on to some new educational level that requires the writer to be able to do certain things. At other times, school authorities require a writing test in order to pressure teachers to teach writing. Still other times, as in a history exam, the assessment of writing itself is not the point, but the quality of the writing is evaluated almost in passing. In any of these assessments of writing, complex judgments are formed. Such judgments should be made by human beings, not machines. Furthermore, they should be made by professionals who are informed about writing, development, and the field of literacy education.

What does this mean for teaching?

Instructors of composition should know about various methods of assessment of student writing. Instructors must recognize the difference between formative and summative evaluation and be prepared to evaluate students' writing from both perspectives. By formative evaluation here, we mean provisional, ongoing, in-process judgments about what students know and what to teach next. By summative evaluation, we mean final judgments about the quality of student work. Teachers of writing must also be able to recognize the developmental aspects of writing ability and devise appropriate lessons for students at all levels of expertise.

Teachers need to understand at least the following in order to be excellent at writing assessment:

- How to find out what student writers can do, informally, on an ongoing basis.
- How to use that assessment in order to decide what and how to teach next.
- How to assess occasionally, less frequently than above, in order to form judgments about the quality of student writing and learning.
- How to assess ability and knowledge across multiple different writing engagements.
- What the features of good writing are, appropriate to the context and purposes of the teaching and learning.

- What the elements of a constructive process of writing are, appropriate to the context and purposes of the teaching and learning.
- What growth in writing looks like, the developmental aspects of writing ability.
- Ways of assessing student metacognitive process of the reading/writing connection.
- How to recognize in student writing (both in their texts and in their actions) the nascent potential for excellence at the features and processes desired.
- How to deliver useful feedback, appropriate for the writer and the situation.
- How to analyze writing situations for their most essential elements, so that assessment is not of everything about writing all at once, but rather is targeted to objectives.
- How to analyze and interpret both qualitative and quantitative writing assessments.
- How to evaluate electronic texts.
- How to use portfolios to assist writers in their development.
- How self-assessment and reflection contribute to a writer's development and ability to move among genres, media, and rhetorical situations.

Bibliography

Anson, Chris M., et al. *Scenarios for Teaching Writing: Contexts for Discussion and Reflective Practice*. Urbana, IL: NCTE, 1993.

Bartholomae, David, and Anthony Petrosky. *Facts, Artifacts, and Counterfacts: Theory and Method for a Reading and Writing Course*. Portsmouth, NH: Boynton/Cook. 1986.

Brady, Laura. "Designing Writing Assignments." 2004. 16 May 2004 <http://www.as.wvu.edu/english/cwe/designing.html>.

Broadhead, Glenn J., and Richard C. Freed. *The Variables of Composition: Process and Product in a Business Setting*. Carbondale: Southern Illinois UP, for CCCC, 1986.

Burke, Jim. "Learning the Language of Academic Study." *Voices from the Middle* 11.4 (May 2004): 37–42.

Gardner, Traci. "Changelog." 5 Apr. 2005. <http://www.tengrrl.com/blog/2005/04/okay-this-feels-like-crazy-question.shtml>.

Glenn, Cheryl, Melissa A. Goldwaithe, and Robert Conners. *The St. Martin's Guide to Teaching Writing*. 5th ed. Boston: Bedford/St. Martin's, 2003.

Hughes, Brad. "Suggestions for Designing Effective Formal Writing Assignments." 2001. 16 May 2004 <http://www.manhattan.edu/services/wac/pages/designing_assignments/suggestions.html>.

Hughes, Brad, Martin Nystrand, Paige Byam, and Tom Curtis. "Informal Writing Assignments." 2001. 16 May 2004 <http://www.manhattan.edu/services/wac/pages/designing_assignments/informal_writing_assignments.html>.

Jamieson, Sandra, and Rebecca Moore Howard. "Checklist for Designing Writing Assignments." 2001. *The Bedford Guide to Teaching Writing in the Disciplines: An Instructor's Desk Reference*. Boston: Bedford/St. Martin's, 1995. 16 May 2004 <http://www.manhattan.edu/services/wac/pages/designing_assignments/checklist.html>.

Johnson, J. Paul. "Ten Tips for Designing Writing Assignments." 2003. 16 May 2004 <http://www.winona.edu/writingcenter/documents/Ten%20Tips%20for%20Designing%20Writing%20Assignments.pdf>.

Kansas State University Department of English. "Expository Writing Program Information for Instructors: Designing Writing Assignments." 2002. 16 May 2004 <http://www.ksu.edu/english/programs/expos/dwass.html>.

Lindemann, Erika, with Daniel Anderson. *A Rhetoric for Writing Teachers*. 4th ed. New York: Oxford UP, 2001.

Mānoa Writing Program. "Designing Writing Assignments." *Writing Matters #1*. 2004. 16 May 2004 <http://mwp01.mwp.hawaii.edu/wm1.htm>.

Mitchell, Diana, and Leila Christenbury. *Both Art and Craft: Teaching Ideas That Spark Learning*. Urbana, IL: NCTE, 2000.

Moore, Cindy, and Peggy O'Neill, eds. *Practice in Context: Situating the Work of Writing Teachers*. Urbana, IL: NCTE, 2002.

Nelson, Jennie. "Reading Classrooms as Text: Exploring Student Writers' Interpretive Practices." *College Composition and Communication* 46.3 (Oct. 1995): 411–29.

———. "This Was an Easy Assignment: Examining How Students Interpret Academic Writing Tasks." *Research in the Teaching of English* 24.4 (Dec. 1990): 362–96.

Northern Illinois University's Writing Across the Curriculum. "How Do You Set Up a Writing Assignment." 7 Apr. 1997. 17 May 2004 <http://www.engl.niu.edu/wac/assprc.html>.

Peirce, William. "Designing Writing Assignments That Promote Thinking." 1998. 16 May 2004 <http://academic.pg.cc.md.us/~wpeirce/MCCCTR/design.html>.

Peterson, Art. "NAEP/NWP Study Shows Link between Assignments, Better Student Writing." *The Voice* 6.2 (Mar.–Apr. 2001). 6 July 2006 <http://www.writingproject.org/cs/nwpp/lpt/nwpr/112>.

Procter, Margaret. "Designing Assignments and Presenting Them to Students." 2004. U of Toronto. 16 May 2004 <http://www.utoronto.ca/writing/design.html>.

Roen, Duane, et al., eds. *Strategies for Teaching First-Year Composition*. Urbana, IL: NCTE, 2002.

Shafer, Gregory. "Standardized Testing and the College Composition Instructor." *Teaching English in the Two-Year College* 32.3 (Mar. 2005): 238–46.

Storms, Barbara A., Anastasia Riazantseva, and Claudia Gentile. "Focusing on Content and Communication." *California English* 5.4 (Summer 2000): 26–27.

Tarvers, Josephine Koster. *Teaching Writing: Theories and Practices*. HarperCollins Resources for Instructors. 4th ed. New York: HarperCollins, 1993.

Taylor, Todd. "Heuristic for Designing Effective Writing Assignments." 1999. Surry CC. 16 May 2004 <http://204.211.175.67/wachome/30sept/matrix.htm>.

Tchudi, Susan J., and Stephen N. Tchudi. *The English Language Arts Handbook: Classroom Strategies for Teachers*. 2nd ed. Portsmouth, NH: Boynton/Cook, 1999.

Virginia Tech University Writing Program. "Assignment Design: Some Considerations." 2003. 16 May 2004 <http://www.uwp.vt.edu/html/online_resources/teaching/olr_menu_01.htm>.

What Can I Write About? 7,000 Topics for High School Students. 2nd ed., rev. and updated. Urbana, IL: NCTE, 2002.

White, Edward M. *Assigning, Responding, Evaluating: A Writing Teacher's Guide*. 3rd ed. Boston: Bedford/St. Martin's, 1999.

Writing@CSU. "Overview: Designing Writing Assignments." 2004. 16 May 2004 <http://writing.colostate.edu/references/teaching/wassign/printFormat.cfm?printformat=yes>.

Writing Study Group of the NCTE Executive Committee. "NCTE Beliefs about the Teaching of Writing." November 2004. 16 May 2004 <http://www.ncte.org/about/over/positions/category/write/118876.htm?source=gs>.

Yancey, Kathleen Blake. "Teacher Portfolios: Lessons in Resistance, Readiness, and Reflection." *Situating Portfolios: Four Perspectives*. Ed. Kathleen Blake Yancey and Irwin Weiser. Logan: Utah State UP, 1997. 244–62.

———. *Teaching Literature as Reflective Practice*. Urbana, IL: NCTE, 2004.

Zemelman, Steven, and Harvey Daniels. *A Community of Writers: Teaching Writing in the Junior and Senior High School*. Portsmouth, NH: Heinemann, 1988.

Zemelman, Steven, Harvey Daniels, and Arthur Hyde. *Best Practice: New Standards for Teaching and Learning in America's Schools*. 2nd ed. Portsmouth, NH: Heinemann, 1998.

Author

Photo by Traci Gardner

Traci Gardner is the online content developer for ReadWriteThink at NCTE. She writes lesson plans, designs interactive student materials, and composes other curriculum and professional development materials. She is also editor of the "Ideas" section of NCTE's *INBOX* newsletter and a contributor to the NCTE *INBOX* Blog. From 1994 to 1999, Gardner was the director of instructional services for the Daedalus Group, where her work included software design and curriculum development for teachers ranging from the kindergarten to the college level. From 1984 to 1994, she taught first-year composition, business writing, and literature in the English Department at Virginia Tech.

Gardner was formerly the NCTE Web manager and chair of the CCCC Committee on Computers in Composition and Communication. She is the editor of the *Engaging Media-Savvy Students Topical Resource Kit* for NCTE and has published articles in *English Journal, Classroom Notes Plus*, and *California English.*

This book was typeset in Palatino and Helvetica by Electronic Imaging.
The typefaces used on the cover were Century Old Style and Novarese Medium.
The book was printed on 50-lb. White Williamsburg Offset paper by
Versa Press, Inc.